CAYCE,
Karma &
Reincarnation

Cover art by *Jane A. Evans*

CAYCE,
Karma &
Reincarnation

I.C. Sharma

Introduction by
Hugh Lynn Cayce

*This publication made possible with
the assistance of the Kern Foundation*

The Theosophical Publishing House
Wheaton, IL U.S.A.
Madras, India London, England

Library of Congress Cataloging in Publication Data

Sharma, I. C. (Ishwar Chandra), 1921-

    Cayce, Karma, and reincarnation.

    Includes bibliographical references.
    1. Reincarnation.   2. Karma.   3. Religion.
4. Cayce, Edgar, 1877-1945   I. Title.
BL515.S45   1982   291.2'37   81-23214
ISBN 0-8356-0563-9 (pbk.)   AACR2

Printed in the United States of America

To *All those*
Who believe in the Unity of all Religions,
Oneness of God and the
Brotherhood of Man

Contents

Preface

In recent years the Western world has experienced a renewed attraction to the theory of reincarnation and the doctrine of Karma, which are fundamentally oriental and particularly Indian in character. Although in the West belief in reincarnation in its crude form of transmigration is as old as Pythagoras, unquestionably reincarnation and its basic precept of Karmic law, are the pillars of the Hindu culture and philosophy, including Jainism, Buddhism, and Sikhism.

I have been dissatisfied with most of the available books on these concepts because they neglect the scientific and philosophic bases of the theories. Hence my desire to place this book, *Cayce, Karma, and Reincarnation*, in the hands of the reader. This book is not an anthology of stories nor is it a narration of events, but strives to be an impartial analysis of the concept of Soul, the purpose and causes of its reincarnation and the ultimate goal of its manifestation in human form. This comparative study of the contemporary Western idea of reincarnation and its Indian counterpart is intended to lead to a better understanding of the unity of all religions, Hinduism, Jainism, Buddhism, and Christianity in particular.

Our approach to the doctrine of Karma is as a law of the conservation of ethical energy, comparable to the conservation of physical energy. The reader will find that there is no need for any technological background, however, to follow the consistent philosophy of life depicted. I hope that this book will be of sufficient general interest to be useful in understanding the essence of religion both as a philosophy and as a practical way of life in our contemporary age of reason, science, and technology.

I consider it my pleasant duty to thank my wife, Mrs. Bhagya Sharma, who typed the original manuscript and gave valuable suggestions on improving the style and on selecting the relevant topics. I also express my gratitude to Dr. Lewis A. Foster, of the College of William and Mary, and his intelligent wife, Anna Grace, for preparing the manuscript in its final form. I must express my thanks to H. Westcott Cunningham, former president, Dr. James C. Windsor, the present president, and Dr. Marshall Booker, the dean, Christopher Newport College, Newport News, Virginia, for providing me the facilities for writing this book. I heartily thank William O. McCabe, M.D., of Forest, Virginia, and his good wife, Annis McCabe, for all the help and encouragement in this mission.

I am also obliged to Hugh Lynn Cayce, director of the Association for Research and Enlightenment, and John Joseph Fenton, president of the Aquarian Age Centre, Virginia Beach, Virginia, for all their facilities and inspiration.

My heartfelt gratitude to Dr. G. S. Mahajani, formerly vice-chancellor of the Udaipur University, now vice-chancellor of the University of Poona, and also to my friend, Dr. R. C. Dwivedi, professor and head of the department of Sanskrit, for his help in making it possible for me to complete this work. I am most grateful to the University of Udaipur and particularly to all the members of the executive committee for giving me the opportunity to go to the United States as a visiting professor and to complete this work. I am obliged to my colleagues in the department, Drs. K. C. Sogani, P. K. Mathur, and K. S. Durrany, for philosophical discussion of the relevant topics. Not least, I thank Mr. Clayton E. Carlson of Harper & Row Publishers for his efforts in the publication of this book.

All scriptural quotations are taken from the Authorized King James Version. Citations for the Edgar Cayce readings refer to case number, reading number, and page number, in the ARE library.

Introduction

The average person who speaks of the philosophy of the Edgar Cayce readings generally refers to the final chapter of *There is a River.*[1] As provocative and as beautiful as it is, we must remember that this chapter was written before indexing of the readings was begun. In considering many of the subjects which can now be discussed in a philosophical frame of reference, we must take into account the availability of a considerable mass of new material from the Edgar Cayce readings. For example, the flesh body itself is the focus of much of Edgar Cayce's concern. In the readings, a very complete philosophy of health is expounded involving a concept of wholeness, or oneness of force—body, mind, soul. On the mind of man, the dream material, as an example, has led to the development of many concepts regarding both conscious and unconscious mental activity. In terms of pure philosophy, Edgar Cayce has a tendency to be extremely pragmatic rather than abstract.

Many people coming upon such basic Eastern teachings as reincarnation and Karma in the readings consider that this indicates an Eastern point of view. They frequently do not go far enough into the readings to realize that rather than just presenting Eastern philosophy, the Edgar Cayce readings focus on a concept of a universal

[1]Thomas Sugrue *There is a River,* (New York: Holt, Rhinehart & Winston, 1942; (New York: Dell Publishing Company, 1967).

Christ-consciousness. Their basic frame of reference is Christianity and the capstone is the figure of Jesus who became the Christ. There are three very popular books on the Edgar Cayce data dealing at some length with the concepts of reincarnation and Karma. Two of these, *Many Mansions*[2] and *The World Within*,[3] were written by Gina Cerminara. *Edgar Cayce on Reincarnation*[4] by Noel Langley presents some new case studies and is the most recent of the three.

Here in *Cayce, Karma, and Reincarnation: A Study of Christian Principles and Indian Philosophies*, for the first time we have a study of the Edgar Cayce data by a highly trained, scholarly, Eastern philosopher. Dr. Ishwar Sharma, chairman of the philosophy department at the University of Udaipur in India and currently a visiting professor of philosophy at Christopher Newport College in Virginia, has not only examined a considerable volume of the Edgar Cayce data, but has set out in this very challenging work to build some bridges between Eastern and Western philosophy, using Edgar Cayce's concepts as planks in the bridge.

During the years of 1969 and 1971, Dr. Sharma frequently visited the headquarters of the Association for Research and Enlightenment in Virginia Beach, Virginia, where the readings are available. He lectured both at ARE conferences in Virginia Beach and in other parts of the country.

Many of his historical parallels and his study of names and terms are exciting and interesting, but in dealing with the concepts of reincarnation, Karma, and grace, and with a major concept in the Edgar Cayce readings, meditation, there are opened up many exciting new ideas which will certainly warrant further examination and study.

It is, I am sure, Dr. Sharma's hope that he will attract the consider-

---

[2]Gina Cerminara *Many Mansions*, (New York: William Sloane Associates, 1950; New York: New American Library, 1967).
[3]Gina Cerminara *The World Within*, (New York: William Sloane Associates, 1957).
[4]Noel Langley *Edgar Cayce on Reincarnation*, (New York: Hawthorn Books Inc., 1968; New York: Paperback Library, 1967).

ation of some of his colleagues in Eastern philosophy in further examination of the Edgar Cayce data. He certainly makes it clear that this is not an exhaustive study nor is it a technical philosophical presentation; but rather the opening of many doors for further consideration. He suggests ways for continued comparative study. It is hoped that both Dr. Sharma and other students of Eastern philosophy will make use of these doorways in future studies. The Edgar Cayce data on religion and philosophy seem to have a universal framework. Here is one scholar who agrees.

It is a great pleasure to introduce this book to a Western audience.

Hugh Lynn Cayce

CAYCE,
Karma &
Reincarnation

1 ❧
Edgar Cayce—A Pragmatic Mystic

The United States of America has long been acknowledged to be a principal influence in the fields of science and technology, and as a result of its development, this nation—so young in culture, so old in the history of democracy—has been accorded international preeminence in political leadership. The true strength of the land however, lies in its people who represent a variety of nations, races, religions and even languages, all making of America a unity in diversity, a harmony in discord, a symphony whose base theme is freedom.

Freedom of thought, speech, and action, and the dignity of the individual are basic for the evolution of democracy and culture. A culture based on freedom is evolutionary, naturally derived, compared with that culture which is authoritatively imposed. The culture nurtured in an atmosphere of freedom emphasizes the development of personality and the growth of the inner and deeper urges of man; a totalitarian culture, externally imposed, subjugates the spirit and annihilates individuality. Evolutionary culture is marked by variety and diversity but has an inner unity; a revolutionary culture has the semblance of unity with a constant internal dissension. The search for truth in an evolutionary culture is unrestricted, offering opportunities to compare and reconcile apparently conflicting areas of knowledge. The result is a pragmatic and realistic philosophy of life, contributing to the maturity of the individual and of the society.

Thus the American ethos, which is an amalgamation of economic, social, moral, and spiritual values, is traditionally a pragmatic, realistic, and dynamic way of life. Since it combines a multiplicity of trends and human interests, it presents a unique working pattern, with a diversity of approach to the unity of the "Final Truth".

The early part of the twentieth century saw a new spirit emerging in the world and particularly in the United States. Specialization in science helped man to understand the mysteries of nature and ushered in an era of dynamic curiosity as opposed to the narrow mechanistic view of the nineteenth century. Along with the interest in the development of physical science and technology, a special interest in psychology, the science of mind, was also apparent in the first decade of the century. This is evidenced by the fact that all the contemporary schools of psychology, such as behaviorism, Gestalt, functional and structural psychology, were organized and developed between the years 1898 and 1912—a period which marked the end of the Victorian era and the beginning of the scientific age. This modern renaissance exchanged ostentatious respect for outmoded traditions for a quest for a new self-discipline and self-culture based on a search for Truth.

In this same period an important breakthrough in spiritual reality, occurred in the United States, through the self-discovery and unique activities of the man named Edgar Cayce, who has been variously titled by writers and journalists as a "sleeping prophet," a "great psychic," a "mystery man." I have designated him neither as a psychic, nor as a prophet, but as a pragmatic mystic.

Pragmatic mysticism is probably a new term, uncoined by any philosopher or theologian. Pragmatism itself is the well-known philosophical approach sponsored by the Americans, Charles Saunders Pierce, William James, and John Dewey. It has been defined as the philosophy of working value, claiming that the verification of a truth consists in its correspondence with existential facts. In other words, for a pragmatic philosopher, the practical applicability of truth has prime importance. Truth must not be contradictory to facts or antagonistic to the successful conduct of life. Applicability of truth therefore, is its proof, making this an empirical and scientific philosophy. It is a view both realistic and rational, with no place for superstitions or prejudice or cynicism, being ultimately an experimental approach, leading to the discovery of an objective, coherent truth. In the present context the term ought to be understood as practical, verifiable, factual, not contrary to scientific findings and logical laws; distinguished from theory, fiction, or myth. Pragmatic truth is one with scientific truth, and even the truth of religion or God, if it is to be considered acceptable, must not be contradictory. This pragmatic method attends truth theories whether they be in the field of theology, metaphysics, science, or logic, evidenced by the entire evolutionary culture of the United States which exists as the living example of the pragmatic approach to truth and life.

The term *mysticism* also needs to be clarified. This word has been misunderstood and misused, especially in the West, frequently being conceived of as a vague and mysterious search for esoteric truth, which a God-commissioned few alone are capable of experiencing. In actuality, mysticism is not represented by the secret revelations of Pythagorean societies, or occult rituals, but is a valid use of psychological potentials which are universally available. In an age of reason, mysticism, as a way of knowing, must be commensurate with other methods of science and reason, such as observation and experiment. However, if observation and empirical analysis cannot disprove the claims of mystic experience, and cannot invent other means of knowing the truths demonstrated by the mystics, they have no right to deny their existence. For what the uninformed may call supernatural phenomena are natural and scientifically verifiable occurrences, which the mystical method can and does verify experientially. True mystic knowledge is always corroborated by facts. Any knowledge or experience which tallies with objective fact and is repeatable under the same conditions, ought to be considered normal and hence, scientific. Such experience and knowledge, though depending on mystical method, should be termed the data of what we have called pragmatic mysticism.

Whatever name we give to the ultimate source of knowledge, or energy, direct contact with that Source obtains an accurate comprehension of truth in every area of human existence—science, religion, philosophy, or history. Since the scientist who has not investigated mysticism has not applied its methods in his area of research, he may shrug at such knowledge and even turn from the very facts which prove its authenticity. But those who do not may find hints of truth which their rationalization overlooks. Let the reader, then, keep in mind an unbiased view of mysticism and then judge for himself the view of the author that Edgar Cayce, in whom science and spirituality conjoined, was not a mere psychic, but a pragmatic mystic.

The word psychic has become very popular, perhaps even notorious, though we know from evidence that there are genuine psychics who exhibit extraordinary powers of telepathy, precognition, clairvoyance, clairaudience, and psychokinesis. These powers are no doubt the effects of the psyche of man in its relationship to some universal unifying vibration. Unfortunately, most psychics are passive recipients. They discover their psychic receptivity purely by accident and most of their psychic revelations are destructive and horrifying, concerned with death, murder, and calamity. The very fact that such persons are the channels solely of horrifying cognitions would indicate that they are passive personalities, since no normal individual would consciously attract such appalling experiences. Such persons are not fully integrated and are in great need of a balanced life. If they could properly attune to the Cosmic Source, they too could develop into pragmatic mystics like Edgar Cayce, but the range of the psychic is limited to one or two areas, while the range of a true mystic is unlimited. Frequently people who are psychic advertise themselves to the world as mystics, but a mystic, being conscious of his voluntary and intensely personal contact with the Highest Source, is not anxious to publicize himself. He does his duty quietly and does not care to exhibit his powers.

Every normal man is naturally attracted to psychic phenomena. What is not often known is the fact that every normal individual is potentially capable of experiencing such phenomena. The application of the method of meditation (which will be explained in a succeeding chapter) is the guaranteed way to the systematic unfolding of psychic powers, as well as an integrated development of the personality, and does not have the disadvantage of producing a passive recipient. It unfolds all the physical, emotional, and intellectual potentialities of the individual, resulting in greater efficiency in all areas of activity. Those who are passive recipients with violent, veridical psychic experiences, may never mature into integrated personalities and may not even know that they have an unbalanced development.

Psychic experiences, accompanied by humility and tolerance, free from egoism and self-publicity, mark an agent who is a mystic, not merely a psychic. A mystic in this sense will be free from all superstitions and prejudices of caste, creed, race, nationality, and even politics. His main purpose is to channel positive vibrations and to contribute his talents to the well-being of humanity without seeking advertisement. Why does he shun publicity? Because he knows that every man is potentially the same and that there is no point in imposing one's experiences on politicians, administrators, and diplomats. He knows that all of them are equally potential mystics and are conducting the affairs of their professions with the efficiency of intuitive knowledge. These people could not have arrived at their place in the world without a developed mystic ability. And so, the mystic must be content to transmit positive energy and let the one in power use his own, more efficient, judgment as his personal responsibility. The psychic, in the same situation, becomes anxious and worried. As such, he cannot be of any real service, because he himself lacks equilibrium, is passive, and does not really know what measures would be proper to avert the projected calamity.

By these definitions, Edgar Cayce was a mystic and not a psychic, because he never sought out publicity by imposing his knowledge on prominent people. Had he pursued popularity, he would not have reached the climax of powers that he did, during the forty-five years of his unique service to the world.

When we consider the contemporary life of Cayce, we find him unexpectedly objective. Unbiased and unaffected by any dogma or sectarian stance, he was the expounder of Truth, which is not the prerogative of any single race, religion, or culture. A psychic often arrives at haphazard conclusions and his ideas are just as often self-contradictory, but the Edgar Cayce readings have remarkable consistency and coherence. Add to that the astonishing range of subjects that they cover—medicine, physiology, psychotherapy, religion, philosophy, history, archeology, astrology, sociology, geology, mythology, metaphysics, evolution, and astronomy—while academically Cayce had no background in any of these areas, and we see why his accuracy and detail in explaining the problems relating to each of these fields have impressed even the specialists. Whatever might be the prejudice of students of the Edgar Cayce material, the presentation of ideas in this book, based on a comparative study, is intended to show that there is a logical consistency and epistemological coherence in what I call his pragmatic mysticism.

The purpose of this book is not to create a halo around the person of Edgar Cayce but to analyze the significance of the man and his work. We will see that his life itself showed how his pragmatic mystical experiences were systematically linked with a purpose, a goal, and a universality which was all embracing and encyclopedic; that his sincerity and enlightenment presented a consistent religious truth, untainted by superstition and blind faith. Consequently, his explanation of religion is neither unscientific nor anti-intellectual, but offers a galvanizing alternative to imagination, guesswork, and narrow dogma, in a rare life of genuine Christianity.

A number of biographies of Edgar Cayce have been published in the United States and the purpose of this account is merely to show briefly how the extraordinary powers of the man developed. Cayce was born in Kentucky in 1877, and we see him unusual, even as a child given to intuitive insights and sensitivity. In his quiet, unassuming way, he was religiously inclined, and in fact, seriously considered the ministry as a vocation. In spite of a lack of academic education, his imagination was keen, his mind intelligent and logical. As he grew older, however, he became socially and religiously dogmatic, limiting his systematic study to the Bible, a study which began in childhood and continued to the end of his life. This rare regularity of scriptural study itself indicates the ingrained religious and spiritual nature of the young man.

Many of the greatest saints and religious reformers in the world have been persons of little academic education, but their lives were illuminated by wisdom and that love which is the most essential characteristic of saintliness and spiritual development. Tulsidasa, the great Hindu mystic poet of the sixteenth century, has remarked, "The rote learning of academic books makes a person a parrot, but not a wise man. One who has really learnt the meanings of . . . LOVE, is undoubtedly a wise man." The wisdom of all ages, the philosophy of East and West and all the religions of mankind are in essence the search for Love—the manifestation of Truth or God. If a person pretends to be wise, religious, or philosophic without practicing love in his life, he is either a hypocrite or a fool. It is a pity that in the modern age, intellectual achievement has been associated with pride and vanity, not with humility and love. According to Indian culture, "Learning gives humility, humility makes a person worthy; worthiness makes him a suitable recipient of wealth; wealth makes a person virtuous and the practice of virtue leads to happiness." Like other great men and saints, Edgar Cayce avoided the limelight throughout his life, demonstrating the humility of the mystic early in childhood, and that potentiality for humility and love drew strength from his continuous study of the Bible.

Cayce's quiet introspection as a child indicated the depth and calmness of his mind, which characterizes saints and sages. This introspection was an innate, not an acquired, trait since his background in philosophy and theology was virtually nonexistent. The only religious or philosophic exposure that he did have was through his personal study of the Bible. This freedom from sophisticated academics was destined to become a great asset as a defense against any suspicion that the readings which he gave while in transcendental trance state were perhaps the expression of his subconscious mind or the articulation of his dormant knowledge. Actually, the unfolding of young Cayce's spiritual powers, from the healing of physical ills to the offering of life readings which dealt with diverse personal problems, thence to the philosophical, theological, and prophetic pronouncements, was so gradual and purposive that his biography presents a uniquely harmonious continuity.

Ever since the literature which describes the maturing of these gifts was brought to the public, it has offered to many unbelieving a renewed faith. To troubled souls and diffident personalities it has offered hope, courage, confidence, and ultimate success in their search for an integrated life.

Edgar Cayce—A Thumbnail Sketch

At age twenty-one, while working as a salesman in a wholesale stationery store, Edgar Cayce was afflicted with an undiagnosed throat paralysis which reduced his voice to a whisper. This illness, probably his first real suffering, became the first step in the revelation of his spiritual potentialities, for when the medical doctors despaired of finding any physical cause for his loss of speech, it occurred to the voiceless Cayce that he might help himself. The question was what that self-help might be, and the answer was a startlingly unorthodox one.

Cayce remembered that in early childhood he had been able to learn the contents of an entire book merely by sleeping with it under his pillow. So, thinking he might find a remedy for his vocal difficulties in this method, he asked a friend, Dr. A. C. Layne, to give him curative suggestions while he dozed. The experiment was a total success and the remedy suggested cured the paralysis permanently.

Thus the discovery of his own mystic power had a personal pragmatic beginning. What Edgar Cayce did not know was that this accidental venture would develop into a systematic approach to human problems, from physical and emotional ailments to philosophical and religious questions of the most far-reaching sort.

Apparently the same Dr. Layne subsequently utilized Edgar Cayce's sleeplike state to procure diagnoses of some of his most difficult cases. This sleep state, reported everywhere as a hypnotic condition, is actually what the mystics call *Turiya Avastha,* or the state of transcendental sleep-consciousness. In this state, which is usually induced voluntarily through the practice of meditation and spiritual self-discipline, the human psyche makes contact with the Cosmic Consciousness and gains knowledge which is not limited by time and space. However, in the instance of Edgar Cayce, his spontaneous mystic ability was the result of the accumulated tendencies of previous incarnations. Since his talents were manifested in pragmatic situations, and since Edgar Cayce's subsequent life readings covered a diversity of religious, philosophic, and spiritual topics, it is more appropriate to call him a pragmatic mystic than a psychic or hypnotic or sleeping prophet.

Nor is the term supernaturalist appropriate, although it was used, since an active membership in the orthodox church of the Disciples of Christ was his only religious background, as is seen in the following anecdote.

About two years after the event of his self-cure, Edgar Cayce was happily married, and a week following, his friend, Dr. Layne, used his psychic talents for diagnosing a difficult case which was reported in a Bowling Green, Kentucky, paper thus:

IN A TRANCE
Bowling Green Man is Able
To Diagnose Human Ills.
Has No Recollection of It
When He Awakes, and Does Not Pretend
To Understand His Wonderful Power

Dr. A. C. Layne, osteopath and magnetic healer was in the city Sunday from Hopkinsville to have Edgar Cayce, the well-known salesman at L. D. Potter and Co., diagnose a case for him.

This sounds peculiar in the view of the fact that Mr. Cayce is not a physician and knows nothing in the world about medicine or surgery. Since Mr. Cayce has been living in the city he lost his voice and was unable to speak a word. He returned to his former home at Hopkinsville and was there treated by Dr. Layne and had his voice restored. At this time it was discovered that Mr. Cayce possessed unusual mediumistic powers and since then he has discovered that by lying down, thoroughly relaxing himself and taking a deep breath he can fall into a trance, during which, though he is to all appearances asleep, his faculties are alert. Sometime ago Dr. Layne had him go into a trance and diagnose a difficult case at Hopkinsville.

The diagnosis proved to be correct in every particular and it was not long until the patient had recovered.

The physicians had been unable to diagnose the case. Yesterday he came here to have Mr. Cayce diagnose another case and it was done in the presence of several people at Mr. Cayce's home on State Street.

The patient is not here, but is ill at his home in Hopkinsville. Cayce went into his trance and then the doctor told him that the patient's body would appear before him and he wanted him to thoroughly examine it from head to foot and tell him where the diseased parts were located.

In a moment more the doctor commenced at the head and asked Cayce minutely about every part of the body. He answered, telling of the location of blood clots, that one lung was sloughing off and detailed other evidences he saw of disease. It was as if the body were immediately before him and he could see through it and discern plainly every ligament, bone and nerve in it.

Dr. Layne was thoroughly satisfied with the diagnosis and when it was complete had Mr. Cayce diagnose several other cases of less importance, and then left for his home and will base the treatment of each case on the diagnosis as given by Cayce.

Mr. Cayce does not know what he is saying while in the trance, nor when it is over has he any recollection of what he said. He does not pretend to understand it and is not a spiritualist in any sense of the word, but is an active member of the Christian Church.

Bowling Green Times Journal, June 22, 1913

The statement that "Mr. Cayce possessed unusual mediumistic powers," in the press report is the attempt of spiritually uninformed newsmen to explain his performance. At the time Edgar Cayce had not gone beyond physical questions and the concept of reincarnation was foreign both to him and to Dr. Layne. Since Cayce was amenable to suggestion in a hypnosislike state, and since Western psychology lacked other terms to describe the level of consciousness which enabled him to perform as he did, it was natural to say that self-hypnosis was the medium of expression. But the very fact that he simply took a deep breath and went into sleep-mimicking trance, weakens the argument for hypnosis, whether induced by Edgar Cayce himself or any other person. The next closest term to describe his sleeping activity, which transcended even his conscious abilities, was trance, and this was the term chosen by the reporter quoted above.

The only real parallel to Cayce's condition is *Turiya Avastha* or the transcendental state of mind, attainable by following the spiritual discipline called yoga, *Samadhi*, or meditation. How this state is available to every individual will be described in a succeeding chapter. This state is quite unlike hypnosis, for one who is hypnotized has a weakened will with all responses under the control of the hypnotizer, whom he always tries to please. Edgar Cayce, during the *Turiya* state was never dictated to by the questioners, his answers always remaining objective and not limited by time and space.

Even in the early readings, as in the one given above, the amazing young man could diagnose ills without the patient being physically present. In the life readings, which relate to such fields as reincarnation, religion, and philosophy, his answers were not only free of flattery but actually shocked the questioners when they contradicted their dearly held beliefs. It seems apparent that Cayce's answers were drawn from an objective source of truth contacted in the transcendental state. Just as the subconscious mind is the basis of the semiconscious dream state and the conscious working state, and just as the unconscious dreamless state is broader than the source of the conscious, the semiconscious, and the subconscious levels, similarly *Turiya* is the basis, source, and even the goal of all. The *Turiya* state has been known and experienced by thousands of yogins and is being experienced by many who follow their discipline. It is not the privilege of a chosen few and is as objective as any other human experience, provided the necessary rules which regulate it are followed.

What Edgar Cayce did was to utilize it for the purpose of solving human problems. This is unusual in the annals of mysticism, for records show that knowledge gained through *Turiya* has only occasionally, in cases of emergency, been used for human benefit.

The so-called psychic ability of Cayce was not a mental eccentricity, some accidental genetic sport. It was undoubtedly an effect of the unlimited power of the human soul or psyche, yet to be gauged by psychology. The inability of psychology to make any remarkable progress in this area is the result of its ignorance of the method of yoga, or meditation, the key to the understanding of spiritual phenomena. The whole life history of Edgar Cayce could serve psychologists as evidence of this observation. Science cannot afford to brush aside the parapsychological phenomena of extrasensory perception, precognition, clairvoyance and clairaudience, for these phenomena as well as that of reincarnation demand answers and scientific explanation. The contention of this author is that all such phenomena are parts of the whole Truth, which is being investigated by the sometimes competitive disciplines of knowledge, including science, philosophy, and religion. They emanate, not from anything physical and spatiotemporal, but from the core of human personality called *Soul* by religion, *"Atman"* by the Hindu sages and *psyche* by modern psychology.

Unconscious and *subconscious* are the terms coined by Western psychologists to suggest the source of psychic phenomena. No matter what the name, it is safe to presume that the source of these phenomena, which apparently transcend time, must itself be transcendental. Let us call it X and avoid all sectarianism and prejudice. This X, which in human individuals is the core of personality and the center of reference, as the agent and the experiencer, must also be the ultimate constituent of the cosmic structure. The art of yoga does not merely presume this, but also demonstrates its truth by the adoption of a technique and methodology which is summed up in the discipline called *Samadhi*, or meditation.

In Edgar Cayce the state of *Samadhi* was spontaneous rather than voluntary, though it was induced by conscious and voluntary effort. Edgar Cayce's later readings emphasized the technique of *Samadhi* or meditation. The volume of the readings had become so vast, varied, and complex that their explanation needed a basis, and meditation was the answer given.

At the start, even Cayce was unaware of the source of his power. He perhaps took it to be a special gift, as people unaware of the law of Karma and reincarnation may do. Although he had helped many patients by his psychic readings, at times he was reluctant to use this faculty, since the virtue of his gift was in question. In 1912 he decided to stop giving readings and settled down in Selma, Alabama, as a photographer. However, unable to refuse his old friends in Kentucky, he visited his old home to give some readings and thus started a remarkable chain of events, for one of these friends, David Kahn, was later to introduce Edgar Cayce, the pragmatic mystic, to thousands of people.

Until 1920, Cayce helped numberless patients through his readings. But his pragmatic use of clairvoyance took a new turn when, in that year, he gave a reading of great accuracy for some oil drillers in Texas. Impressed by their success, Cayce and his friend Kahn ventured into the oil business, motivated by a desire to finance the establishment of a hospital devoted exclusively to the diagnosis and treatment, through the readings, of hopeless illnesses.

It was undoubtedly an altruistic mission, oriented towards a very pragmatic use of Cayce's gift. However, the spiritual basis of his talent was as yet undisclosed to the men. Had this venture been fruitful; had Cayce and Kahn been successful in raising funds for the establishment of a hospital through the discovery of oil fields, the life and work of Cayce would have served a fine humanitarian cause. But, perhaps fortunately, the readings concerning oil did not bring the men any financial gain. In the year 1923, Cayce started giving what are now called "life readings," thereby introducing a new dimension to his accomplishments. It was in Dayton, Ohio, in that year, on the request of a wealthy printer, Arthur Lammers, that Edgar Cayce penetrated into the depths of metaphysical and philosophical knowledge.

Edgar Cayce had no philosophic background at all and certainly no acquaintance with Hinduism, Buddhism, or Western metaphysics. Since Cayce was an unsophisticated, orthodox Christian, a fundamentalist with blind faith in the literal meaning of the Bible, the topic of reincarnation was naturally foreign to him. Nevertheless, in a reading given on the request of Mr. Lammers, he referred to the previous incarnation of the person whose reading he was giving.

When he returned to his waking consciousness and read what he himself had stated about reincarnation, he was deeply shocked. After a sleepless soul-searching night, torn by worry, he agreed to give further readings according to the plans of Mr. Lammers. For, Edgar Cayce, the devout and sincere student of the Bible, who had read that book at least once every year, could find no reference which refuted the notion of reincarnation. Furthermore, on closer examination of some of the passages of the Old and New Testaments, he found that the fundamental principles of Christianity could not be made wholly intelligible without the theory of reincarnation and Karma. Having arrived honestly at his decision, Cayce subsequently gave thousands of life readings in which he traced present tendencies of persons to many past incarnations. In the law of Karma, which alone explains the basic Christian tenet, "As you sow, so shall you reap," he found the explanation of the existence of evil and inequality in the world, which according to all great religions, is dependent upon a Supreme Being, who is neither evil nor imperfect.

If the law of cause and effect is at work in external physical nature, human nature cannot be immune to its workings. The law of Karma, then, is the law of ethical or volitional causality for the soul on earth. Without the acceptance of the two basic principles of Karma and reincarnation, the concept of the soul as an immortal entity, with a relationship to a just and good God, would be a fiction and delusion.

These two principles, which will be detailed in a later chapter, give coherence and intelligibility to religion, redeeming it from blind faith and anthropomorphism. They bridge the gap between science and religion on the one hand and metaphysics and logic on the other. The Edgar Cayce readings, which have not merely mentioned instances of reincarnation, but have also guided many individuals to make use of the acquisitions of their past lives to achieve success in the present, testify to the pragmatic use of the law of Karma.

Edgar Cayce must be regarded as a mystic because the knowledge which poured out during his trancelike state had no direct empirical background. It was an enclyclopedic approach to human problems, ranging from medicine and therapy through cosmology, astrology, and theology, to history, sociology, geology, and geography. However, this knowledge, although coming from a source beyond intellect, was corroborated by facts and was consonant with contemporaneous discoveries in the respective fields.

The Sanskrit words *Karma* and *Akashic*, which appear frequently in the course of many of the statements of Edgar Cayce may be unfamiliar to some readers but their use does not surprise anyone conversant with Hindu philosophy. Medical doctors might still wonder at the exactness of the terms that Edgar Cayce used in diagnosis and prescription, since he had no empirical background in medicine. But anyone familiar with the systems of Hindu philosophy and the method of yoga, would not be in the least surprised to find the seer consistently and accurately using appropriate language for any field, for they know that truth is objective and will be the same whether it is known through empirical study or the intuitive method of mysticism.

We are presuming here that mysticism is neither mythical nor miraculous. Mysticism, truly practiced, does not merely exist, but is the system of proof of the existence of clairvoyance, precognition, telepathy, and other extrasensory perception as real experiential data.

In this age of science, reason, and analysis, explicit terms are necessary. Somehow the words *intuition*, *mysticism*, and *spiritual* have been so poorly understood in the West that academicians are reluctant to use them in their writings, and scientists say that they are unable to explain the phenomena under the known laws of physics, chemistry, and biology. Some parapsychologists, on the other hand, have applied statistical methods to their investigations in these areas and have formulated hypotheses regarding, among others, psychokinesis and extracerebral memory, but miss the core of the problem in trying to control the external situation without controlling or conditioning the self, or soul, of which all these phenomena are the effects—in short, analyzing the symptoms without looking for their genesis. It is a sad fact that in scientifically advanced Western culture everything *other* than self, or soul, has been studied objectively. Self, or soul, must be postulated as a premise in order to give a scientifically systematic explanation of the so-called psychic and supernatural, which apparently contradict physical laws. But no research has been done to gauge the inner nature of man, supposed by some to be a mechanical outcome of a chance combination of atoms and electrons. The soul force, generated by self, and more subtle and faster in motion than any physical force or motion now known to physics, is an unknown and unexplored phenomenon to Western science and philosophy.

When psychic phenomena are either disregarded as nonexistent, or neglected as abnormal because not all individuals seem to experience them, superstition and blind faith are fostered. All religions have stated that the soul is nonmaterial, unlimited by time and space, and is more than mind, consciousness, and intellect. All physical phenomena are within time and space, and all sensory knowledge is explicable within the framework of mathematical measurement and mechanical causation. Hence, physical phenomena and sensory knowledge must have a spatiotemporal source, and that source must necessarily be material. But telepathy, precognition, clairvoyance, and clairaudience are effects which defy mechanical causation. The obvious solution to this problem is that the objective factor causing these must be an extraspatiotemporal factor common to all human individuals. The concept of soul provides the answer to the quest for that factor.

We must bolster science and challenge superstition. We must carry out a dispassionate study of all that has been designated as supernatural, abnormal, and mysterious. Such an approach compels us to start with the concept of the transcendental self or soul. If we adopt this scientific attitude we see that the supernatural will not be unnatural, but intensely natural. The *ab*normal will not be *non*-normal, but most accurately normal, and the mysterious will not be mystery, but symmetry and harmony made explicable by the laws of human nature.

Mysticism, therefore, should not be confused with supernaturalism and abnormality. There may be greater or lesser degrees of mystical experience, depending again on the laws of human nature, which include the law of Karma and the theory of reincarnation, the law of love, and meditation or yoga. But what has so far been considered to be the privilege of a chosen few is actually the potentiality of all human beings.

We have striven to maintain a catholic, unbiased attitude throughout this study, endeavoring to produce not merely another biography or narrative, but an honest probe into the nature of the human soul. We will consider its basis, its purpose, its evolution and its destiny, as it is bound up with the physical, spatiotemporal, dynamic world of constant motion on the one hand, and the noncorporeal, transcendental, eternally stable, infinitely conscious, infinitely potent, and infinitely blissful world of the Spirit on the other.

2 &

Man's Search for Eternal Truth

The propulsive force behind world civilization has been man's un-quenchable desire to probe—from the outer reaches of the universe to the depth of his own personality. To fathom the secrets of external nature and the experiences of the inner self; to glimpse the intimate relationship of spatiotemporal destructible matter and transcendental indestructible psyche has been the motivation for our cultural evolution. This innate urge to understand the immutable laws of natural forces and to overcome the limitations in human mastery of space and time, disease, old age and even death, is indicative of the presence in finite personality of that which, in essence, is infinite and eternal—the Soul, *Atman*, Logos.

The analysis and comparison of the vast fields covered by the world's scientists, sages, and seers are studies in themselves. But here we are concerned mainly with man's efforts to understand "Truth" which is eternal, yet which appears in varied forms, in different relations and combinations, in varying degree and dimension, in the physical, mental, intellectual, and spiritual experiences of man.

Facts suggest that the gradual progress of human knowledge in the fields of science, religion, and philosophy, which seems to be bringing man nearer the whole truth, is hinting at the integration of all the specialized branches of knowledge into one organic pattern, the Eastern concept of unity in diversity.

There is no question that specialization, which is a recent development in science and technology, has been of tremendous practical use to man. The present progress of culture and human society, the growth of social, political, and cultural institutions, could not exist without the specialization of research. Because of specialization, contemporary society has the advantages of technology for a happier life, free from want, hunger, and disease. Because of specialization, even the average man in today's affluent society has all the amenities of comfort and ease. Because of specialization in physical, biological, and social sciences, unprecedented progress has been witnessed in our time. But that same specialization has created the urgent need to coordinate and compare discoveries of all the particular disciplines, and to disseminate the findings through public communication media. For whatever synthesis has been done has pointed to one exciting fact—that all the ways of the search for truth are converging at one point.

Man is very slow in recognizing this unity of truth and teleology of evolution, being inclined to overemphasize differences at the cost of the intuitive vision of unity. Even so, glimpses of the eternal Truth, whether experienced by scientists, philosophers, sages, or mystics, have again and again indicated that the Ultimate Truth is One.

Edgar Cayce's testimony to this fact is a unique contribution to comparative research in many areas. A careful study of the thousands of readings reveals how the physical, mental, ethical, metaphysical, and spiritual realms are intimately interdependent and that their truths are ultimately unified.

We are fortunate that this spiritually awakened clairvoyant, this potential prophet, lived in our time. For the period was a crucial one —crucial for hope and despair, for progress and deterioration of human institutions and ideals.

The first half of the twentieth century, during which Edgar Cayce attained prominence, was a transitional period of human history. It was a period when political institutions developed rapidly and two world wars brought havoc as well as hope—in the atomic destruction of 1945 on the one hand, and the coincident establishment of the

United Nations Organization on the other. It was a period during which the greatest democracy of the world experienced the worst economic depression and also reached a height of affluence and prosperity. It was a period during which occurred the vile atrocities of autocrats and dictators, as well as the emancipation of nations whose freedom had been trampled for centuries by imperialistic ambition.

Many of these events had been accurately predicted by the Edgar Cayce readings—an indication of the specific quality of his message. His genius analyzed the present predicament of the human race, diagnosed the disease, discovered the cause, and suggested the remedy. It was pure accident that the discovery of his latent spiritual powers, which definitively displayed the eternality of final Truth, began with the diagnosis of physical disease. But this accident is significant in that a deeper study of what he expounded during his trance state convinces us that the purpose of his life was to diagnose the genesis of humanity's suffering and to prescribe the remedy which would lead to lasting peace.

Thus we have the paradox of a man with no medical training, with no more than a seventh-grade education, a photographer by profession, who spent his adult life verbally projecting pictures of the cosmos, the evolution of the world, the development of civilization, the relation of man and Maker, and thereby revealing the secret unity in all existence.

The importance to the modern Western world of this revelation of reincarnation, of Karma, of religious unity, of love as the basic remedy for all ills, cannot be underestimated. It occurred at the most opportune time in human history, particularly with regard to science, philosophy, and religion, the disciplines which have traditionally devoted themselves to truth search.

We need merely consider briefly the history of philosophy, which originally encompassed the areas of science and religion, to see how the tower of Babel has been reflected in the history of Western thought. The castism in these three areas of Western culture (which is applauded as more progressive and dynamic than Oriental) is a strange phenomenon. Though philosophers and scientists disavow tenacity in truth seeking, a large majority in the West have refused to give up routine methods of research and have adhered to theories, even at the cost of facts. The same is true of many Western theologians, who have not shed conservatism even though honest attempts have been made to reinterpret the theories of philosophy and religion in the light of scientific discoveries. At the other extreme, some have repudiated even the basic truth of religion, while creative scientists are accepting its plausibility. The basic fact, of course, is the existence of God, as Supreme Reality, as the Unmoved Mover, immanent as well as transcendent force, the ground of all that has being. It is really the greatest anomaly of our age that in the West there are Godless theologians affirming the death of God as the doctrine for modern times.

At the very face of it, the statement that "God has died in our own time" and that this death of God is "ontological," a real death of His Being, is logically absurd. One cannot use the term *God* and also state that He is mortal. It is not clear what the godless theologians mean by the term God when they make their assertions, or what their motives may be, but sensational, provocative statements, even illogical ones, are sure attention getters. Actually, this anomalous attitude is more than likely the outcome of that trend in Western culture which has effectively isolated philosophy, science, and religion from one another.

Research and scientific discovery in the second half of the twentieth century illuminates this blundering bifurcation of knowledge.

Like historians in general, historians of philosophy are prejudiced by one theory or another and the account they give is partial and biased. Only by studying ancient Greek thinkers from original sources and reserving judgment, can we discover their errors. A dispassionate study of the philosophers of Greece shows that their sole purpose was to understand the nature of cosmos and the meaning of human life. For them, especially the great thinkers—Heraclitus, Pythagoras, Socrates, Plato, and Plotinus—cosmos and man, God and individual soul, had intimate relation with each other. In order for them to understand the purpose of human life or its meaning in the cosmos, analysis both of the physical world and of the relationship of human consciousness to God was necessary. Even Heraclitus, often wrongly depicted as the philosopher of purely physical change, had the passion to look behind change and to assert that Logos, the universal principle of harmony, is the final principle. Enthusiastic modern philosophers have frequently neglected this theological aspect of ancient Greek philosophy. But the ancient philosophers were no mere theorists. They existed prior to the prejudices of naturalism, monism, pluralism, realism. Their main interest was the expression of their innermost experience.

Today it is popular to say that Socrates was the founder of a theory of knowledge, but, unlike Plato, had little concern for metaphysical systems. The prejudice of these observations becomes apparent when Socrates' words are studied and one finds that he only expressed the visions, and ideas, which were the outcome of his thinking, meditation, and intuition. His life demonstrated more than a theoretical belief that man's goal was to rise above worldly limitations. His courageous speeches at the time of his persecution, his refusal to be intimidated or to attempt to escape punishment, are facts of underestimated significance. Contemporary historians of philosophy overlook the great emphasis which Socrates laid on "taking care of the soul," and the importance of his spiritual experiences—the source of his own beliefs and the source of inspiration to his pupil, Plato.

Intuitions and dreams guided Socrates throughout his life. He refused to exchange poison for exile by pleading guilty, not simply because he thought it unethical, but because of a prompting from his divine source. Plato's dialogue, "Phaedo," which records the last words of Socrates in prison, expresses his life's spiritual and metaphysical basis. The pupils are astonished at the courage and calm which the teacher displays, as he emphatically dwells on the immortality of the soul and declares that death is not evil. He says that a philosopher must die happy in the cause of truth, because only by death can he hope to attain the greatest good in the other world, for to Socrates pure knowledge is attained when the soul separates from the body and when God Himself is pleased to release the individual. Throughout his discourse, there is no doubt that the intellectual approach of Socrates, in the clarification of concepts and the significance of virtue, was inspired by his inner spiritual urge for the purification of the soul.

Plato's philosophy has been accepted as primarily spiritual, perhaps even mystical, by most scholars, and we note that the foundations laid by Plato still stand strong. In the areas of metaphysics, sociology, political science, and even theology, the profundity of his thought and the depth of his insight are unsurpassed, and the remark of Whitehead that "the development of Western philosophy is but a series of footnotes to Plato" is not without foundation. However, what most Western philosophers have neglected is the fact that Plato's theory of "recollection," in which the soul has the potentiality for all knowledge within itself and all learning is merely remembering, implies strongly the theory of reincarnation of souls.

Plato's greatest contribution to philosophy is the clarification of the relationship between the spatiotemporal world and the supreme transcendent God. For Plato, the soul is like a two-faced mirror. On the one hand, it reflects the world of objects and on the other hand, the transcendental reality, God. Origen, the great Christian Platonist, accepted the theory of recollection, and Plato was the source of inspiration to many other Christian thinkers, as the expression of inner experience gave added dimensions to the intellectualized Truth. The source of that experience is the godlike core of human personality, the basis of everything that exists. In other words, a true philosophy can only arise from spiritual experience, because spirit is the essence of all existence. The term *spirit* is applied to the infinite basis both of human personality and of the cosmos. All great philosophers have had access to the power of the spirit, and have tried to express their experiences without reservation, as did Plato. Such an expression should be judged in its wholeness, not analyzed or isolated from its context, as contemporary scholars attempt to label Plato a realist, or an idealist, or a monist, or a combination of all these ideologies. We should never forget that the eternal truth is not bound by any limitations or isolated viewpoints.

Partiality does not enter the theories and speculations of a truly great philosopher, for he experiences the truth, living it constantly—while discussing, while arriving at conclusions, while thinking, feeling, and willing. What is projected through his intellect and reasoning is this vision of Truth, which arises from his soul. It is a spark of intuition, produced by the contact of human personality with the Cosmic Current. The conscious mind, through the mediacy of the subconscious, receives its inspiration from the unconscious psyche, which is in direct contact with universal Truth, and glimpses the wholeness of truth. For this reason the findings of such a philosopher cannot effectively be studied from any particular theoretical point of view, for the philosophy is always inspired by the spirit and is inseparable from religion. This special characteristic of unity of experience has been neglected by contemporary historians, who have been misled by their own overemphasis on analysis, differentiation, and extreme specialization.

Plotinus, who is called a neo-Platonist, is another victim of the historians of philosophy. It is claimed that Plotinus's teachings were the culmination of ancient Greek and Roman philosophy, and our study of the history of philosophy might lead us to such a conclusion, since Plotinus followed chronologically Plato and his immediate successors. But this culmination was not a mere summary of what the previous writers had stated. It may be granted that Plotinus's ideas derived their inspiration from Plato, whose philosophy he thoroughly studied. But, at the same time, we cannot isolate him from the great cultural and philosophical influences of the Christian period 204–269 A.D., during which he lived. The greatness of his teaching, however, does not depend on his study of Plato nor on the observations of contemporary Christian traditions. Plotinus's philosophy was primarily the outcome of his personal inner experience and his spiritual development. His own intuitive experience, his meditation, the glimpses of the divine light, led him to his fundamental convictions, concluding that God is the source of all existence.

Plotinus's cosmology reveals the presence of individual differences and plurality of souls in the spatiotemporal world, emanating from one God, who is Himself infinite and undifferentiated. This One is also the Supreme Good, identified with the light above light. Beyond this however, he tried to avoid the use of any positive concept to define God, lest it conceptually limit Him. Human soul individuates from the World Soul, which itself is an emanation from the infinite God. Before being incarnated, the soul was in a state of constant contemplation of the eternal Nous (Mind), and had complete knowledge of the Good. Having separated from God and descended into the material world, it is now on its journey back to God and passes through various births in this ascent towards its Supreme Source. In the state of ecstasy, the soul is raised above all limitations and merges with the Soul of God. Only thus reunited with its source can the soul reattain true knowledge. These ideas cannot be labeled the mere summary of a theoretical study of Plato or Aristotle on the part of Plotinus. Rather, they are the expression of empirical inner experiences arising from the link of this individual consciousness with the cosmic current. His strong living philosophy was not merely a feeling, but an integrated whole of knowing, feeling and willing—a unitive dynamic and experiential pattern.

Toward the close of the Greek and Roman period and the beginning of the medieval period, a similar amalgam of spirit and reason, intuition and intellect, religion and philosophy, appeared in Saint Augustine. But subsequent philosophy in the Middle Ages was subordinated to theology, and reason, in the Aristotelian sense, was subjected to faith. Aristotle had admitted, with Plato, that reason in man was the reflection of the divine element, but stressed its practical utility in understanding the physical world. He purposely neglected the spiritual aspect of human personality and, thus, started a trend toward the dichotomy between the empirical and spiritual worlds. As a result, theologians in the Middle Ages, fearing secular intellectual growth, subordinated philosophy to religious tradition. Prior to this time, philosophy had been inspired by the spirit of true religious experience. The attempt of the theological philosophy was to derive inspiration from philosophy to establish a stronger foundation for traditional religion. A multitude of logical proofs for the existence of God were propounded, and Aristotle's theory of causation was commissioned to prove that God is the final and efficient cause of the world. Philosophers in their eagerness to justify theology, ignored the fact that reason is finite, and no intellectual exercise can comprehend completely the nature of an infinite God.

Reason can neither prove nor disprove the concept of God as Final Cause, any more than it can resolve whether the hen or egg is first cause, but the conflict between reason and faith had a twofold effect on the history of Western philosophy. First, it brought about the suppression of objective reason and the reduction of philosophy to a secondary status of handmaiden to religion. In other words, the impossible attempt was made to give secular reasons for spiritual truths with the stipulation added that in matters of conflict, religious authority be accepted as final.

The second effect, which was the outcome of this liaison, was the invention of the theory of double truth—the truth of reason and the truth of faith—nurturing a split personality which lingers even now in Western philosophy. However, any recourse to the segregation of the truth, the division of basic reality into any kind of dualism, is bound to be abortive in the end. For the concept of "unity in diversity" is not purely intellectual. It is the result of dynamic spiritual experience which academicians have always lacked.

In the ensuing reaction to the suppression of reason by the medievals, modern thinkers enthusiastically infused a spirit of freedom from all religious presuppositions into an independent philosophical discipline. The methods of honest doubt and pure analysis were advocated by such men as Bacon, who said that dispassionate induction would lead to the objective knowledge of the external world, which would ultimately lead to the control of nature. So far as the knowledge of the changing, moving, physical world of time and space is concerned, his observation was flawless, and his forecast has come true. But the hidden power of the human psyche, lies unexplored and unutilized, awaiting another Bacon to advocate a method, not of analysis, but of intuition.

Bacon also encouraged the dualism of science and religion, philosophy and theology. He inspired the British empiricism of Hobbes and Hume. Both of these radical philosophers can be recognized as the pioneers of skepticism of the Western world. This skepticism is, to a great extent, responsible for the radical trends in modern theology.

The philosophy of rationalism opposed the empiricism of Hume, but passed through various phases, beginning with Descartes, who has beautifully defended the concepts of self and God. It culminated in Kant, the great German philosopher of the modern period. Unfortunately, Descartes, who seems to have had some background in spiritual experience, overemphasized the dichotomy of body and mind, and matter and spirit. Kant was a more profound thinker than Descartes, but had the disadvantage of being purely academic in his attitude, although he did at times affirm faith in spiritual concepts. His greatest contribution in dispelling the skepticism of Hume was to give practical and ethical arguments for the problems of the existence of God, the freedom of will, and the immortality of the soul. However, he divided the domains of knowledge into two water-tight compartments—the domain of science and the domain of religion—and his insistence on maintaining the theory of double truth was disastrous.

Kant's claim that we cannot do without the concepts of God and soul, freedom of will and immortality, but at the same time, we cannot prove their existence in the realm of pure reason, has given Kant the appearance of an agnostic—withholding final judgment on the existence of the spiritual realm of God and soul. However, he went on to say that we should not reject the notions, since these concepts must be accepted on pragmatic grounds as necessary presuppositions. The same philosophic attitude is held by many American pragmatists.

Pragmatism is the philosophy of "working value." Its criterion of truth is practical utility—we accept an idea as true as long as it works, as long as it satisfies our need. Thus, God may or may not exist in reality, but we accept the concept of God because we cannot live successfully without it. Pragmatism may be a very successful philosophy for the economics of human life, but in the realm of spiritual experience, it is a great handicap, since this experience is a link between the world and spiritual truth, and without an inner realization of this truth, mere pragmatic tests fail to give any insight. One of the great weaknesses in religion is the acceptance of God as Father and Person, on primarily pragmatic grounds. God or Truth, as an impersonal basic reality, is accepted in the realm of science on the same basis.

Science remains contented with a disinterested search for truth, until ultimately it is faced with ethical problems. It must also settle certain issues with religion. Psychology is forced to consider the psyche, which embraces the conscious, the subconscious, the unconscious and the paraconscious levels of mind. Similarly, the physicist's concepts of infinitude and omnipresence conflict with the notion of a personal God. Pragmatism ultimately fails to resolve these issues. This results in the dichotomy of truth and opposing theories which distort the truth. The radical theologians deny God by declaring His death. The radical traditionalists stick to the literal interpretation of the Holy Bible, shutting their eyes to any scientific truth. Thus, they bring about an absolute schism between science and religion, philosophy and theology.

Edgar Cayce was able to avoid this extreme polarization of thought because his contact went beyond both the finite world and the personal nature of God to their mutual infinite source. As a keenly intelligent, well-founded Christian, he was never unfaithful to his religion. Actually, he has, through his work, strengthened the scientific and philosophic foundations of a true universal Christianity. His philosophic, metaphysical, and ethical notions are consistent with religion and coherent with scientific and philosophic theories. He was not an academic philospher, nor a radical traditionalist, but his readings are an answer to both. His notions are not the mere outcome of reason, but they tally with the concepts of great philosophers, spiritualists and scientists, because they come from his psyche, attuned to universal knowledge. He could draw upon that source of spiritual energy which is the core of man's being. Wherever a man searches for truth, the recognition of that truth always emanates from the soul, the infinite aspect of the finite personality.

When the intuition is honored, and when the inner experience corroborates the external observation, the diversity is understood in its right perspective. Differences and duality are not abolished, but an insight into the underlying unity weaves a coherent and consistent pattern into the differences. Truth is then established as an organic whole of various interrelated parts, which are neither mutually exclusive nor absolutely independent. Reality is fundamentally one and essentially eternal.

3 ❧
Science, Religion, and Philosophy

Since science, religion, and philosophy are human disciplines, human pursuits, involving human goals and discoveries, the source of their origin must lie in the nature of man, in his mental and psychological constitution. Although religion emerged prior to philosophy and science, the three have coexisted in some form from the beginning, generated by man's threefold nature of knowing, feeling, and willing, or, curiosity, the urge to love, and the will to control nature. Science, the disinterested search for truth about natural phenomena, is really nothing but man's attempt to satisfy his own curiosity. Man's religion, the acceptance of the love of God and of fellow human beings, issues from the emotional aspect of man. Finally, philosophy aims at understanding the ultimate truth about the cosmos and the purpose of human life. It is man's intellectual effort to effect a relationship between knowledge and feeling, science and religion, and to understand their interdependence.

The three disciplines are not mutually exclusive, just as the activities of knowing, feeling, and willing in man's behavior are not isolated. Animals may largely apprehend their environment through sensation, but man's cognition is reflective, his sensations are meaningful, conveying objectivity and significant pattern. Man's feelings go beyond immediate pleasure and pain; they are complex wholes of feeling, instincts, and emotions, all organized by reflection into a pattern called sentiment. Lastly, man's actions are not merely impulsive tendencies, but more often than not, a cool, considered, voluntary act of will, which essentially involves reflection and reasoning.

All lower animals have awareness, affection, and strivings in a rudimentary form, but these activities, without reflection, remain undeveloped. And so, animals have not invented a science, adopted a religion, or propounded a philosophy, for man's reflection, love, and volition, involve a subtler understanding. They originate from the soul or self which is the core of man. All knowledge that carries the idea of unity and organization, all feeling that urges man to love rather than hate, and all action which impels him to manifest good will, owe their function to that source. The powers of soul or self, unlimited by time and space, psychoanalysts like Jung have called the *unconscious*. The word *unconscious* is a negative term, but it implies the positive content of that unlimited psyche, of which consciousness is just one infinitesimal part. We justly admire consciousness because it is through that function that we know, feel, and will, but we should not forget that the psyche is wider than these three manifestations of the soul.

The fact is emphasized because the unity in all human experience is due to the self-conscious subjectiveness of man, termed ego, or personality in its conscious aspect. But beyond that, beyond even the subconscious, there is a coordinating unity, whose source merely includes ego as one of its products. Ego reflects that true self, or soul, which gives unity to the aspect of psyche beyond the conscious. When the individual ego establishes connection with the soul, even the involuntary functions of breathing and circulation come under its control, as we see in the highest level of meditation, *Samadhi*.

Samadhi, translated only approximately as trance, literally means unification or balance of all physical, mental, and intellectual experiences and activities of the self, through subjugating them to the pure self or soul. This description of *Samadhi* is the result of thousands of years of research by the yogins of India. The yoga system, formulating the systematic technique of attaining *Samadhi*, was elaborated by the great sage Patanjali, in the eighth century B.C., though its origin is certainly much older. Edgar Cayce arrived at the same conclusions as the great sages of ancient India, which have been confirmed by thousands of others since. His readings are convincing, not simply because predictions have subsequently been corroborated, but because they represent a direct contact with the Cosmic Consciousness and eternal Truth.

This brief definition of the word *Samadhi*, the highest stage of meditation, is based entirely on the study of Indian philosophy, the yoga system and the personal observations and demonstrations of living yogins. Edgar Cayce, describing meditation in his readings, said it is the "attuning of the mental body and the physical body to its spiritual source . . . For ye must learn to meditate—just as ye have learned to walk, to talk, to do any of the physical attributes of thy mind as compared to the relationships with the facts, the attitudes, the conditions, the environs of thy daily surroundings" (281–41).[1]

This quotation indicates that truth, being one, cannot be distorted, and the conclusions of different researchers will ultimately agree. The apparent unity of human personality suggests that man's three limited characteristics, knowledge, feeling, and volition, are originally associated with the source of unity of both the conscious and unconscious self, and that although consciously we consider the three separately, they are actually interrelated and even simultaneous. It is impossible to remove all thought from feeling and emotion, or all sentiment from thinking and volition. Man as a self-conscious personality experiences all three processes as one whole, and when in the state of *Samadhi*, the soul is at its highest level, the trinity of the experience is fused into one complex whole. This state transcends all triads of time, space, and causality; past, present and future; knower, known, and knowledge; reason, faith, and intuition. Hence the trinity of science, religion, and philosophy is no less a "unity in diversity" than the trinities of reason, faith, and intuition; birth, evolution

[1]Numbers appearing after Cayce material designate documents on file in the Association for Research and Enlightenment (ARE) Library, Virginia Beach, Virginia.

(reincarnation), and resurrection (life eternal); Father, Son and Holy Ghost. All of these, in a very deep sense, represent and manifest the same unconflicting truth, with God as the source. It is the fallacy of segregating truths which has been responsible for confusion and chaos in modern man.

Without the concept of universal, consistent truth, man becomes a fractured personality. The scientist says that the truth of the laboratory is different from that of the church. The minister affirms that God is irrelevant to scientific findings and that such truth differs from that of the Bible. Strangely enough, this anomalous acceptance of the theory of double truth—spiritual and secular—existing like parallel lines without interconnection, is held by many Western intellectuals even today, despite the fact that the latest researches in science have confirmed the orderly force in biological evolution, mental expansion, and intellectual growth in the universe.

As an example, we know that the sun is the center of our solar system with the planets revolving around it, forming our largest known physical pattern. The smallest form we know, the atom, is a perfect replica of the solar system. Both have a nucleus as the center of gravity, with the atom's electrons moving like planets around it. The repetition of the pattern in interstellar systems is the stamp of an intelligent guiding source of order and uniformity.

Research in other physical sciences equally points to a harmony where every particularized organ of the human body works for the whole, and even a simple injury to the organism recruits the process of healing in every part of the body. Henri Bergson has given countless examples from the biological world to prove that every part of the living organism works for the system so purposively that one is forced to believe in the existence of a creative intelligence, or élan vital behind the evolution of life. These discoveries, plus the success of science in controlling nature through knowledge of immutable laws, and all evidence testifying to uniformity in causation, reaffirm that the originator of the dynamic, creative cosmos is not any caprice, but a purposeful and intelligent, eternal Being.

Edgar Cayce referred to the thread of unity which runs through the world when he spoke of the emotional disturbances of his physically suffering patients. He referred to a patient as an "entity," affected by planets, past lives, previously acquired skills, at the same time that he diagnosed upset stomachs and damaged kidneys. Science aims at understanding the laws of causation, claiming that predictions in nature are logically possible as a result of the interconnection of forces. If this claim is true, Edgar Cayce did not deviate from the scientific method in citing the influence of the past and of planets on man. He simply demonstrated the inseparable tie between science and religion.

Sophisticated scientists and historians of science write of religion's beginning in superstition, blind faith, and mythology. They allege that religion started with fear, with ghosts and spirits, animism and ancestor worship. Primitive man, they say, worshiping sun and moon, serpent and lion, was ignorant of the roundness of the earth, its rotation and revolution, and they proudly picture Copernicus, Galileo, and Newton redeeming man from the nonsense preached by religious dogmatists. They stamp the ancient religions, which date back to the centuries before Greek philosophy, as self-deception and illusion, not realizing that, in fact, the scientist of today is merely corroborating truths discovered by men of religion at least four thousand years ago. In spite of the antiquity of the evidence, the truth is that it speaks of the motion and revolution, not only of the earth, but also of the sun, solar system, and galactic center, and gives names to the orbits of these systems. Let us examine then, this oldest theory of the universe.

This five-sectional-branch theory of the universe was based on the concept of *Prajapati*, the Supreme Master of Creation. Some Western scholars of Vedic literature have translated *Prajapati* as a personal God, the Supreme Being of the Hindu religion. There is no doubt that creation, preservation, and destruction of the cosmos, in one basic reality called Brahman, have been accepted as the three functions of God or *Prajapati*, but to interpret this Creator as a God having personality is absolutely incorrect. The term *Deva*, which is added to *Prajapati* in the Vedic literature is derived from the root *Div*, as in "divine," to shine or to illumine the sky. Thus, *Deva* means a shining entity or a force of nature which has light as its basis, as when Jesus says that he is "the light of the world." The Vedic literature gives the adjective, *Deva*, to all natural forces and entities, and since all these are dependent on the Supreme Force of *Prajapati Deva*, all of them share in the *Devatva*, or divinity.

Prajapati, the presiding deified force, is the core of all evolutionary existence. The Vedic literature states, *"Prajapati* remains in the center of everything; it is immanent, unborn and yet, sprouts forth in a multifarious manner; the wise know the secret of this core of *Prajapati* and also know that all the levels of creation in the universe are founded on it."

The same writing theorizes that earth, moon, sun, galactic center, and cosmic center are the five sections of one branch of the universe that is ours, and that numberless such universes exist in the cosmos. The earth *(Prithavi Devata)* revolves around the sun *(Surya Devata)* on its revolving orbit *(Kranti Devata)*. Secondly, the moon *(Chandra Devata)* revolves around the earth on its orbit *(Daksha Vritta)*. The sun, the third section of the universe, is also not stationary, but it revolves around another center accompanied by its planets. This center, around which our solar system and many other systems are revolving, is the familiar *Vishnu*, galactic center, preserver of life, sun of suns. The galactic center further moves around the cosmic center *Prajapati*, the creative force.

In more modern language, the ultimate source and ground of creation is one infinite Being, indestructible, dynamic and immanent, unaffected by the evolution of the universe. As the dynamic agent, it becomes the Creator of the universe; as the immanent Being it becomes the personal, omnipotent God (the Father of the Bible), the object of worship and communion.

This cosmology of the Vedas is in turn related to its philosophy of the nature of man, social systems, and ethics. Man is a miniature universe. Or, metaphysically speaking, "Man is the image of God," and as such, parallels the universe, the body representing the earth element and the mind, or consciousness of emotion, representing the moon. The third element, more subtle than mind, is the rational aspect of human personality, or *buddhi*. This intellect is the manifestation of the sun, solar energy. It is only beyond these three systems of the microcosm that man's soul reflects both the galactic and cosmic centers of the universe.

Man's *Atman*, or soul, according to the Vedas, combines the eternal *Avyaya*, *Purusha*, and *Mahan Atman*, or the invisible pure spirit and man's impersonal unconscious self. Pure *Atman* reflects the original immanent manifestation of God, the cosmic center, and from it originates all levels of reality. *Mahan Atman*, or the great self, is man's galactic center, comprised of unconscious tendencies inherited from seven preceding generations and transmitted "unto the seventh generation." The composite of these aspects is the *Jiva Atman*, soul, or as Edgar Cayce appropriately titled it, "the entity."

It is difficult for modern scientists to accept the fact that their carefully corroborated knowledge of the systems of the universe were known to ancient India. But actually, the theories were even further related to human psychology and ethics, which declared that man's healthy integration is based on a balanced development of the body, mind, intellect, and soul. Man's corporeal being is developed through *Artha*, the economic value; *Kama*, the satisfaction of desires, particularly sexual, through conjugal love, is necessary for normal emotional growth; *Dharma*, the ethical value, or duty, renders service to one's fellowman and nourishes the human intellect. Lastly, having recognized the soul as the center of human personality, the Vedic psychology suggests that for spiritual development man must hold *Moksha*, eternal spiritual liberation, as the highest goal of life.

Yoga, which is known to the Western world as primarily a physical discipline, was originally taught as the method of obtaining this *Moksha*. It is the system of bodily and mental exercise used in attuning to one's own innermost self, and is as essential for a healthy and normal life as is food for the body, the mind, and the intellect. We will see that the Cayce readings adapt the disciplines of yoga and *Samadhi*, or meditation, for the identical purposes of the Vedic teaching.

In modern psychology, intellect and mind are not separated. If a threefold nature of personality is tentatively accepted, we have body, mind, and soul as the three major aspects of the individual. The physical man and the universe is the concern of science; mind or understanding is the occupation of philosophy, and the soul is normally supposed to be the business of religion. However, it is evident that no isolation of the three is even possible. The three must cooperate to do justice to the nature of the complex human personality.

Although the approaches and techniques may differ, the truth of science, the truth of religion, and the truth of philosophy are one, and the goal must be the same. Scientists do not disagree about the nature of the atom. They do not quarrel about the effects of radioactivity. Truth in science is not the monopoly of any one nation, race, or culture.

But God, the common ground of all religions, frequently has been monopolized by a view of religion, narrowed by nationality, race, or culture. In an objective consideration, if God is omniscient, can He be limited to one language? If omnipotent, can He not manifest Himself in the form most desired and understood by the devotee? If omnipresent, is He not equally present in the temple, mosque and church?

At the core of every religion, the unity of the spiritual element in man and the oneness of God as the ground of all existence have been evidenced by highly developed souls like Edgar Cayce. They have experienced God as the final and Supreme Truth, universal and infinite, an all-pervading power and an all-revealing Being. Because there are infinite manifestations of that power through infinite media, the human approach to the apprehension of God is diverse. The scientist "seeks God" through analysis of the physical world, finding uniformity in nature, but also an infinitely receding frontier of knowledge, which ultimately leads him to the threshold of man's spiritual nature.

The spirit or soul is the unity from which the diversities of the physical, biological, and social aspects of man derive. It is the inner-most nature, whose essence is the subjectivity of the agent and experiencer. Human matter is the outermost nature, objective in the sense of being passive and extended in time and space. It is not an agent, but the object of an agent, which is the soul. Matter is not the knower, but that which is known; not the experiencer, but that which is experienced.

Man's superiority over the other beings lies in the fact that he is conscious of his subjectiveness. He knows that he is the knower. He is self-conscious. Nonliving matter is presumed to be unconscious, with consciousness only dormant. In the subconscious activity of plant life, consciousness dreams. Only at the animal level does con-sciousness become manifest, experiencing perceptual, emotional, and instinctual behavior. But in man, consciousness reaches the level of *self*-consciousness, making him a free agent. He has freedom of will, the power to choose between alternatives through the exercise of reason. It is man's self-conscious soul which makes him different from the nature of other creations.

Religion differs from science because its emphasis is on the soul. Yet science is also a search for the soul, a search directed from outside inward. Science would not exist if it had not been activated by the self-consciousness of the soul. Nor would religion exist without that same self-conscious transcendental nature of man.

Religion aims at the understanding of the inner nature, just as science aims at understanding the outer nature. Religion experiments with the soul in the spiritual laboratory, as does science in its physical laboratory. Science arrives at the universal knowledge of matter, which transcends geographical, cultural, and racial boundaries. Reli-gion, which aims at the universal knowledge of the soul, transcends all boundaries of sect, denomination, and church. Thus science and religion have a similar stimulation and approach to truth, with a similar goal of catholicity. There is no rational antagonism between the two disciplines. On the contrary, as Edgar Cayce confirmed in the broad scope of his readings, science and religion are interdependent and interrelated. The truth is one, the function is one, the goal is one.

4 ❧
Bridging the Gulf

How can the gulf between science and religion be bridged? Logically, there should be no disjunction, but we have seen that, particularly in the West, there has been a longstanding conflict between the two. When a new scientific theory was offered, such as Darwin's theory of evolution, the church often denounced it as atheistic. It is the function of philosophy to clarify issues, but contemporary philosophy itself has created misunderstandings, by devoting itself to such methods as linguistic analysis, with little interest in metaphysics and ethics. Religion, too, has lost its place in today's dominant academic trends as philosophy in the West becomes rigidly technical, and irrelevant to the problems of human society.

In its beginnings Christianity abhorred philosophy, and today philosophy derides religion. Tracing the history of this antagonism may help us to understand its genesis.

That most histories of Western philosophy have been written in the twentieth century, from the contemporary philosophic viewpoint, is a significant fact, as modern philosophers have tried to read their own theories into the writings of the ancient Greeks. The designations of monism, pluralism, materialism, and idealism are concoctions of modern philosophers trying to fit their ideologies to those philosophers who had simply expressed what they had experienced.

As one example from history, the first Greek philosopher, Thales, known as the father of Western thought, is categorized as a naturalistic philosopher. The modern scholars have exalted him as their high priest because he was presumably the pioneer of secularism, whose greatness lay in breaking loose from theological and religious biases. It is true that Homer and Hesiod, who preceeded Thales, were poets and mythologists, attempting to answer questions about cosmology in terms of mythology, anthropomorphism, and animism, and Thales contributed greatly to the scientific approach in his designation of the physical element, water, as the basic stuff of the universe. He is hailed unrealistically however, as the patron of philosophy, secularism, and rationalism because he was a realistic thinker, free from all nonsense about spirit, soul, and divinity. It is ironic that Thales is considered the first philosopher for his repudiation of the spiritual attitude, whereas Plato, who is unsurpassed in all areas of philosophy, was one of the most profoundly spiritual thinkers in the history of man.

Born in approximately 625 B.C., Thales flourished as a philosopher in Miletus, in Asia Minor, until his death in 545 B.C. A man of dynamic personality and versatile genius, he was considered one of the great sages of ancient Greece and even the philosophers and historians of his own time referred to the contribution of Thales in the fields of astronomy (then astrology), politics, engineering, meteorology, geometry, and navigation. His wit and repartee was full of depth and wisdom. Once, when asked why, since he believed that there was no difference between life and death, he did not kill himself, Thales answered sharply, "Because there is no difference." At another occasion, he stated that the happiest man is "he who enjoys a healthy body, a resourceful mind, and a calm disposition." He considered the knowledge of one's own self as the most difficult task, and giving advice to others as the easiest one.

Although it is generally felt that the greatest contribution of Thales to philosophy was the view that water is the primary substance out of which all creation springs, yet to neglect his other works, in the field of metaphysics, would be an arbitrary abridgment of his theological and metaphysical views. Lacking a written record of his philosophy, scholars frequently select one aspect of his thought, based on the evidence of Aristotle that Thales was a practical philosopher, and claim him to be a physicist.

Aristotle stated that the four salient features of Thales' philosophy, which Thales himself held basic, were that water is the basic principle of all things; that earth floats on water; that everything in the world is full of gods; and that the magnet has a soul because it can move iron. It is, however, assuming a great deal to conclude from this that Thales was not a metaphysician, or that he did not inherit the Greek tendency of regarding the basic reality as something spiritual, invisible, and transcendental. But contemporary, science-oriented philosophy does neglect the last two statements of Aristotle as unimportant vogue which Thales inherited from current religious beliefs and emphasizes the first two statements to prove that Thales was an empiricist, a physicist, and a scientist—not a speculator or metaphysician. Even if subsequent evidence is overlooked and Aristotle is accepted as the only source of our knowledge of Thales, it is prejudicial to neglect the important references to gods, which symbolically represent cosmic forces and to the soul, the essential feature of which is dynamism and motion.

Aristotle pointed out that Thales considered water to be the basic substance, because moisture is the cause and sustenance of life by which even the gods of mythology swore. In almost every book on the history of philosophy, these remarks of Aristotle are overemphasized and Thales is dismissed after mentioning that he was a physicist and that his greatest contribution was his avoidance of anthropomorphic terms. But we cannot ignore the fact that Thales was a metaphysical philosopher and that he used the term "god" in a metaphysical and naturalistic sense, as a force of nature and not as a person.

Significantly, Aristotle lists the philosophy of Thales in his metaphysics, not in his classification of science, contending that Thales considered soul as a motive force and "gods" as an immanent reality, present in the whole universe. In the words of Aristotle, "From the stories that are told of him it would seem that Thales conceived of soul as somehow a motive power, since he said that the magnetic stone has soul, because it sets a piece of iron in motion."[1] Thus even if the concept of water as the basic substance was borrowed by Thales from the Olympian pantheon, why could the borrowing not have been based on a symbolic interpretation of mythological terms? That a symbolic interpretation was not unknown is obvious when Aristotle says, "Some say that soul is diffused throughout the universe; and perhaps that is what Thales meant in saying that all things are full of gods."[2]

This important remark suggests that the Indian concept of Brahman, the immanent and transcendent God of the Vedic Upanishads, may have been known in Greece by the seventh century B.C., and the third proposition of Thales indicates that he believed in the universal immanence of a spiritual principle, as the Upanishads have affirmed. The lack of firsthand knowledge of Thales' ideas makes it impossible to establish his belief in an immanent spiritual element in the universe. But it seems consistent to accept Thales as a metaphysical philosopher who accepted a spiritual, dynamic, but naturalistic, element as immanent reality, as did the later Vedic writers of India.

The essence of the Upanishadic philosophy is that the physical elements including air, water, and indefinite matter—whether called "apeiron" by Anaximander, or "chaos" by Hesiod—are in themselves insufficient to explain the world process, for the explanation of evolution is incomplete without accepting the invisible dynamic force, present not only in living beings, but also in nonliving matter like the "magnetic stone," as Thales observed.

A commentary by Aetius on Thales theory of creative motion says, "Thales declared that God is the same as mind in the universe, that this all is ensouled and full of spirit, and that a divine moving power pervades the elemental mosisture. He was the first to declare that the

---

[1]Philip Wheelright, *Presocratics*, (New York: Odyssey Press, 1966) p. 47.
[2]Ibid.

soul by its very nature is always in motion, and indeed is self moving."[3]

The testimony from the Latin sources confirms that Thales used the word "god" symbolically and meant by it the controlling dynamic force or motion responsible for the evolution of the universe. The testimony states, "Thales of Miletus, who was the first to study such matters, said that water is the first principle of all things, and that "god" signifies the mind which forms all things out of water."[4]

Just as the term *god* is a double symbolism, the term *water* has two meanings in this context. In one sense water is the liquid, which modern science tells us is composed of hydrogen and oxygen. It is in this sense that water is regarded as the source of life on this earth by Thales. But when he states that the universal mind, the dynamic, all-pervasive force, creates all things out of water, the term water has a different connotation. Here it stands for the moist principle. This vapor, or element, which for want of the word, could not be designated as gaseous, appears to be some universal entity. The Vedas also state that the creation of the universe started with the interaction of *Agni* (heat principle) and *Soma* (moist principle), and these principles are the cause of the generation of the primeval nebulae which evolved into the material stellar system. A more thorough study of Thales and his parallels with Eastern thought shows us the father of Western philosophy as a far more complex thinker than has sometimes been assumed.

In this single example from ancient Greek philosophy, we may conclude that originally philosophy and religion were not mutually exclusive. To substantiate that claim, we can study another important philospher, Pythagoras, whose work is an outstanding example of philosophy based on religion and who was the foremost propounder of the theory of reincarnation in the West.

Even the so-called skeptic philosopher, Heraclitus, cannot be un-

[3]Ibid., p. 50.
[4]Ibid., p. 51.

derstood without reference to God, whom he designated as Logos, the controlling, intelligent principle of all apparent change and conflict in the world of space, time, and causality.

Socrates, who preferred death to abandoning his search for truth, theorized that the world is guided by benevolent forces. His entire philosophy centers around the goal of "taking care of the soul." We have already referred to the deep theological basis of philosophy and the philosophical interpretations of Socrates and Plato. Even Aristotle propounded the idea of "Unmoved Mover," which was adopted by Saint Thomas Aquinas as the basis of his argument to prove the existence of God.

Stoicism held a basically religious belief in Logos as the Alpha and Omega of the cosmos, with Logos equivalent to God as the Supreme Being, the Prime Mover, the cause, the process, and the goal. It is the intelligent principle which controls and harmonizes the evolution of matter, mind, and soul. The soul is the image of God, with reason as its guiding principle in man, corresponding to the universal Logos, and man must harmonize his emotions to live a life in tune with the Cosmic Logos, God.

The Buddha, in India five hundred years before the Christian era, represented a somewhat different tradition. Disturbed by the sufferings of humanity, the Buddha wanted a direct prescription for salvation and freedom from disease, old age, and death, which he found in extreme pragmatism. He was even silent to the questions of the existence of God and the immortality of the soul, neither affirming nor denying, although both of these doctrines were implied in the acceptance of the reincarnation of soul and the concept of Nirvana or spiritual liberation. In the last days of his life, the Buddha admitted that he had not revealed everything. Sitting near a *sinshup* tree one day, he placed some leaves in front of his disciples and said, "Are these leaves the whole of the sinshup tree?" "My dear disciples, just as the handful of these leaves are not the whole tree, similarly the truth that I have told you is not the whole truth. I have only expounded to you the most essential elements of truth, necessary for

Nirvana. I have not told you many other things purposely."

The approach of Jesus Christ was similar, for two reasons. First, his immediate audience could neither grasp the subtlety of metaphysics, nor believe in such explanations if Jesus had attempted them. They were simple, uneducated people, steeped for centuries in a false interpretation of religion. In the Gospel of John, Jesus says that he cannot reveal to them everything concerning heaven, because they are not even prepared to believe in the things which he says concerning this worldly life. The false notions, superstitions, and vices that had gradually made the existing religion a closed system, could not be remedied easily. Jesus also knew that the metaphysical principles would gradually be understood and that an elaborate system would only cloud his teaching. So, he referred to metaphysics only allegorically and instead emphasized the law of "Grace," which is the essence of Christianity.

Contrary to some teaching, Grace itself is not absolutely a free gift, for if it were, there would be no need of awakening Christ-consciousness in people. Had it only depended on blind faith, Jesus Christ would not have told his followers to be perfect as the Father, and to love their enemies, in godly manner, as God showers His love on the virtuous and the vicious alike.

When Grace leads to the dawning of wisdom, the knowledge so acquired is beyond all concepts, all language, all expression. It is transcendental joy. But it is a real experiential state of living and existence. It is here that the philosophic basis of Grace must be understood. To say that there was no metaphysics involved in the notion of Grace is to neglect the teachings of the Bible.

In one such passage Jesus refers to his disciples as being one with himself and himself as one with God. He says, "They are not of the world, even as I am not of the world. Sanctify them in thy truth; thy word is truth" (John 17:16–17). The meaning of the term "word" here is purely metaphysical because the first verse of this Gospel of John identifies word (Logos) with God, ontologically and metaphysically. When Jesus refers to his own self as being not of this world, he is not alluding to his physical body as Jesus Christ, the son of man. He is clearly referring to his spiritual abiding aspect of divinity, a divinity he also presupposes in his disciples and in all human beings. The word (Logos) is potentially present in every individual and it is through the awakening of this Logos (the God or Christ image) that human beings can be united with God. Jesus makes this clear: "Neither pray I for these [disciples] alone, but for them also which shall believe on me through their word: that they all may be one; as thou, Father, art in me, and I in thee, that they also may be one in us: that the world may believe that thou hast sent me" (John 17:20–22). Here, God is one metaphysically and the believers of God (whose wisdom has been awakened through Grace) would also be one metaphysically. Other passages from the Bible substantiate this point. The quarrel between philosophy and religion, whether it be Christianity, Hinduism or Buddhism, is groundless. On the other hand, the teachings of Jesus without reference to their implied metaphysics are unintelligible.

The main reason for the antagonism between early Christianity and the philosophy of that period is historical. The so-called pagan philosophy was Greek and Roman. The sophisticated Romans, who hated the Jews, were uncompromising philosophers. The Stoic philosophy, the main line of paganism, had deteriorated. The wisdom which was the keynote of Socrates, Plato, and Aristotle had become interchangeable with intellectual pride, and philosophers at that time had contempt for the common man. Thus, early Christianity felt justified in opposing philosophy, for fear its adherents might be corrupted.

However justified the fears of the time may have been, it would be wrong to condemn philosophy as a whole. Hindu philosophy, for example, is much older than Greek and had a very broad outlook from the beginning, advocating humility as the main characteristic of real knowledge and wisdom. Love of God, based on self-surrender to His supreme will (because God is considered the source of all love and mercy), leads to the awakening of wisdom and true knowledge in man. Had early Christianity come in contact with Hindu philosophy (which Jesus refers to as the "other fold"), perhaps the antagonism between philosophy and religion would not have grown in the West. Edgar Cayce's readings in this regard do not indicate any conflict between the two. Significantly, Cayce always mentions God as the Maker, the Master, the First Cause, the Creative Force. He has clearly pointed out that the sole purpose of human life is God-realization. The Cayce readings elaborate the metaphysical aspect of the Bible, particularly that of the Gospel of John, Luke, and Matthew, showing that there is no antagonism between wisdom and love, between philosophy and religion.

Even when Cayce was not specifically asked about the one basis of reality, the First Cause, which he identifies with the "Creative Energy," he conveyed this impersonal concept of God, which is the source and goal of individuated souls. This philosophical notion of God is, at the same time, a religious notion and is not opposed to the personal aspect of Creative Energy.

In reading 5753–1, Cayce says, "Each soul that enters, then, must have had an impetus from some beginning that is of the Creative Energy, or of a first cause. What, then, was—or is—the first cause; for if there be a law pertaining to the first cause it must be an unchangeable law, and is—IS—as 'I AM that I am!'" (5753–1). Note that this statement of Cayce was made in response to a request for a discourse on reincarnation. Before making the above statement as the premise to the conclusion of the fact of reincarnation, Cayce remarked, "Yes. In giving even an approach to the subject sought here, it is well that there be given some things that may be accepted as standards from which conclusions—or where parallels—may be drawn, that there may be gathered in the minds of those who would approach same some understanding, some concrete examples, that may be applied in their own individual experience" (5753–1).

Cayce was certainly not an academic philosopher, and was not intentionally setting forth any particular metaphysical theory. All of these statements were given when he was in the self-imposed hypnotic state, the state of yoga, attuned to the cosmic source of all knowledge. Moreover, he was an individuated soul making an attempt to express the truth about the infinite in conceptual and finite terms, which should "be accepted as the standards from which conclusions—or where parallels—may be drawn." The very fact that Cayce identifies "Creative Energy" with "The First Cause," which is regarded as "unchangeable law," indicates that the basis of all existence is one. All activity he declares to be the manifestation of the Creative Energy. In his words, "Hence in the various spheres that man sees (that are demonstrated, manifested, in and before self) even in a material world, all forces, all activities, are a manifestation. Then, that which would be the companionable, the at-oneness with, the ability to be one with, becomes necessary for the demonstration or manifestation of those attributes in and through all force, all demonstration, in a sphere" (5753–1).

When we come to understand this subtle explanation of the evolutionary cosmos, the inseparability of philosophy, religion, and science becomes apparent. Man, as a creative being, is the highest manifestation of the Creative Energy. Cayce also points out that the goal of the individual soul, or entity, is his re-union with the First Cause. He says: "Hence man, the crowning of all manifestations in a material world—a causation world, finds self as the cause and the product of that he (man), with those abilities given, has been able to produce, or demonstrate, or manifest from that he (the soul) has gained, does gain, in the transition, the change, the going toward that (and being of that) from which he came" (5753–1).

Here Cayce is referring to the source from which man came, not as a person, but as "that." Man is the "crown of creation," "the image of God," because the Creative Energy attains self-consciousness only in human beings. If both the original source and final goal of man is God, as the Creative Energy, it might appear that Cayce was biased toward a Stoic philosophy or an absolute pantheism, with the annihilation of the individual soul. But closer examination shows that what he is relating is an expression of the truth of unity in diversity

—the coexistence of the personal and impersonal aspects of God, who can be approached through the law of love or of Grace. Mark how Cayce's philosophy differs from Stoicism and from paganism, which was shunned as an anti-Christian ideology.

First, Stoicism has no concept of love or Grace, which Cayce indicated is supreme, but instead it emphasizes effort and the exercise of intellect. Grace is the effect of human effort, but that effort is specifically the exercise of the free will to choose love and to reject hatred. That intentional love is an attitude, by the whole man, of firm belief in the goodness of all, with humility as the basic virtue. The intellectual effort of the Stoics is unconcerned with the tenderness of the human heart, and is untouched by humility. The proud, sophisticated self-respect for intellectual man in Stoicism, is the opposite of Christian love, which Edgar Cayce has sponsored as the cure of all ills and as the sole gateway to the development of the soul toward at-onement with God.

Secondly, Stoicism believes in an unrestrained fate with no freedom of will to overcome the finitude of the soul by invoking Grace. The entire metaphysics and ethics of Cayce's philosophy, on the other hand, culminates in the law of Grace.

Man is superior to all nature, in being essentially a self-conscious, subjective agent, the voluntary chooser. Man is a spiritual being, endowed with a transcendental soul, not merely an entity, governed by laws of natural selection and competition. Man's self demonstrates the reality of a factor which unifies the diverse physical and intellectual elements of his personality. All thoughts of truth, as the basic unity of knowledge; all feelings of love, as the unifying force of emotion; and all actions of virtue and justice, as the cementing power of goodwill, owe their existence to the soul. The soul, in empirical experiences, is the conscious mediating agent, as it is the harmonizer of subconscious activities of human personality. Just as the soul is the source of equilibrium in the physical and intellectual domains, so is God, as the Creative Energy, the harmonizer and the preserver of the cosmos. The Stoics' weakness was ignorance of the law of love as the agent of harmony between the individuated Logos and the cosmic Creative Energy.

The self-control, rationality, and ethical rigor of the Stoics are not enough to awaken the spiritual potentiality of man. The law of love enlightens the individual, eliminating egocentric emotions, and leading him to universal love by direct contact of the soul with God. Through love, true understanding of the nature of man and the universe resolves differences, removing apparent contradictions, because it emanates from the unifying soul.

Intellectual comprehension by itself tends to be divisive and analytic because it classifies and compartmentalizes facts. Lacking the intuitive faculty, it fails to grasp the unifying, integrative nature of truth. The apparent contradiction between the personal and impersonal nature of God is due to this failure and is logically as well as psychologically false.

Emphasis on the impersonal aspect of God maintains the image of God as the supreme and inexhaustible source of the world. The great philosopher, Spinoza, pleaded that God should not be considered as a person or even as a designer or an architect, for to do so means that He is limited by the objective world. He must be limited by His own design and by the material used in building a designed world. God has infinite attributes, accepted by religion in the affirmation that God is omniscient, omnipotent, and omnipresent. Spinoza insisted that consciousness and extension, or, mind and body, are just two of the infinite attributes of God, who is the Supreme Source, the Supreme Substance in which all beings have their existence. We cannot refute Spinoza's argument that by reducing God to a person only, we degrade Him and deprive Him of infinitude. God cannot be a person only; cannot be referred to as *He* in this meaning, for taken literally, we might conclude that God is limited to the male person of Jesus Christ.

Hinduism has avoided this error, by designating God as Brahman, the Being, both immanent and transcendent, male and female. Brahman is the origin of the spatiotemporal world as well as being the uncaused, unborn and unmoved mover of the constantly caused, and constantly evolved and destroyed, cosmos of living and nonliving entities.

But this notion of the impersonal Supreme Being, does not preclude the notion of God as a Supreme Person, as the creator, preserver and destroyer of the world of names and forms. Spinoza, or any philosopher who regards God as the ultimate substance, source and goal of all being, must also admit that such a Being is omniscient, omnipotent, and omnipresent. Once these are recognized as characteristics of God, the contradictions between the personal and the impersonal, finite and infinite, immanent and transcendent aspects of the Supreme Being automatically vanish.

Accepting these attributes, then the religious notion of God as the Supreme Person, who enters into intimate relationship with His devotees, logically follows. If a man becomes God-intoxicated, as Spinoza did, but considers God as a Person, then God may appear to him as Krishna, Jesus Christ, or Mohammed, whomever the devotee has accepted as the image of God, for if we deny God the ability to appear as these personifications, then that God can be neither omniscient nor omnipotent.

On the same grounds, a truly consistent and logically acceptable religion cannot assert that God is the Supreme Being and yet only a Person. It is true that God is immanent in the world, but this does not mean that the Supreme Being is coextensive with the world. He is within the world and yet is more than the world. He cannot be limited by the physical, mental or rational personality, because matter, mind, and rationality do not exhaust the nature of God.

Perhaps immanence and transcendence are the only two conceptions of God, the Creative Energy, which may be apprehended through an analytical perception of science or philosophy or the intuitive and spiritual experience of religion. The Infinite Being of philosophy, the unfathomable Truth of science and the immanent and transcendent God of religion, are one and the same Entity, perceived through the three dimensions of man's nature, knowledge, feeling, and volition.

Although I do not believe in anthropomorphism nor in anthropocentrism, I emphasize the nature of man because I consider the human element of subjective self-consciousness to be the highest manifestation of God. It is in this sense that man has been regarded as the image of God and the crown of creation. Science considers man to be the highest rung on the ladder of evolution. Whether our approach is scientific or philosophic or religious, the nature of man as an amalgam of extension and consciousness, finitude and infinitude, matter and spirit, must be recognized to contain the whole truth.

The key to the riddle of the universe lies in the nature of man, who is both the researcher as well as the subject of his research. He is mortal as well as immortal. His physical body is subject to decay and death, but his psyche seems to survive time and physical annihilation. The theory of reincarnation and the doctrine of Karma attempt to explain this apparently paradoxical constitution of man. Before examining these two foundation stones which support science, philosophy, and religion, let us examine the nature of the soul and the proofs of its existence according to Hinduism and the philosophy of Edgar Cayce.

5 ❧
The Nature of Soul

Man is "the image of God" in his superiority to all other finite creations. He is not the image of the absolute God of pure form, but of the cosmic deity manifested in the spatiotemporal world of universes and their varied inhabitants, of which man is the crown in the hierarchy of being.

The details of this hierarchy will be discussed in the chapter on Divine Descent or *Avataravada*. Our purpose here is to point out that man as the image of God is both finite and infinite—finite in body and infinite in soul. Nearly all religions believe in soul as the noncorporeal support of the corporeal body and as something which survives the physical death of the individual, but only Hinduism has elaborated extensively on the nature of that soul. In most religions the soul and its immortality is taken for granted, its existence accepted on faith, and no study made of existence after physical dissolution. Moreover, immortality is often attached to the resurrection of the identical body as the necessary vehicle of the soul.

Why then, if this were so, did Jesus Christ emphasize that a Christian must be born again? Immortality obviously is not the immortality of the body, but of the soul, and survival is not that of the physical members, but of the spiritual self. This condition is implied in the statements of Christ, who was concerned mainly with the ethical and spiritual regeneration of his people. He was more pragmatic than metaphysical in his speech, but whatever metaphysics we can derive, clearly point out that the soul is incorporeal, God is Spirit, and man as the image of God is immortal in soul, but not in body.

How, then, does man survive? Historically, it would seem that all references to reincarnation as a possible life continuity were erased from scripture by a number of antagonistic ecclesiastical councils between the third and thirteenth centuries A.D. Lacking any theory of the soul and its functions in the embodied and the disembodied states, resurrection and eternal life in traditional Christianity have remained vague doctrines. In this vacuum, the dogmas of hell and heaven, the wrath of God and unpardonable sin, have been constructed to enforce the religion of the Prince of Peace, who primarily preached complete self-surrender of man to the God of Love.

My contention is that the theory of reincarnation is not only not antagonistic to Christianity, or to any monotheistic religion believing in God as a loving Father, but is unavoidably essential as the basis of the immortality of the soul and resurrection. Christianity, like Hinduism and Buddhism, would be self-contradictory, or a mere blind faith, without reincarnation, which affirms that soul is immortal and that it has not merely two dimensions, but three—past, present, and future. Western philosophy and theology are at least partially indebted to Edgar Cayce for this contribution to Western culture.

Before elaborating the theory of reincarnation and its logical foundations, as well as the contribution of the Edgar Cayce readings, let us review the evidence from the *Bhagavad-Gita*, the quintessence of Hinduism. The *Gita* propounds the philosophy which was preached and practiced at least five thousand years ago by the Hindus and continues to be practiced today. It accepts God, both as immanent and transcendent, as a Supreme Person and also as the Being beyond personality. He is the object of worship as a Creator, Preserver, and the goal of the entire cosmos. He is Master, Supreme Witness, Father, and Ultimate Refuge. God is one, omniscient, omnipresent, and omnipotent. Man, as the highest divine manifestation in the visible form, is in constant quest of his source, God. Or, as St. Augustine wrote: "Thou hast created us for Thyself and our heart knows no rest, until it may repose in Thee."[1] The purpose of human life is to seek God through the path of true knowledge, love, and service irrespective of occupation, or caste, or creed, or culture.

The *Bhagavad-Gita* does not preach renunciation or asceticism, but it does exhort every individual to utilize his earthly existence to evolve the soul to its greatest potential by subordinating all thoughts, feelings, and actions to the love of God and man. Having reached a stage where he is completely dedicated to God and where the light of God is seen reflected in all creatures, man continues to perform his life's duties without indulgence or attachment and with full consciousness of God. This highest stage of spiritual liberation or self-discovery actually foreshadows the soul's eternal life, attained after physical death. But to reach such a state the soul passes through numberless incarnations, progressing towards perfection, till it becomes worthy to receive the highest Grace of God.

The supremacy of the law of Grace is not in question, but to merit it does require effort, knowledge, and the voluntary practice of love, requirements which the readings of Edgar Cayce abundantly confirm. This highest stage described in the *Gita* is not easily attained. Among millions of persons, a few seek this path, fewer still persist and the fewest reach the goal. With the same potential, ultimately all souls are destined to attain it, some early, others late, because all are pilgrims to the Holy Destination, but some are indolent, some are drawn to alluring sidetrips, some move slowly and only a few are enthusiastic marchers. There are stopovers in the long march towards the final goal and these stopovers are the "many mansions" of scripture. The freedom of will granted to all individuals influences the choice of speed, hesitation, or even retreat. There are some advanced souls, who, having reached the goal, rejoin the march and help others along the right path. This aspect of the divine guidance will be covered with the subsequent study of divine descent. We are confined here to reincarnation and rebirth of the soul. These

[1]St. Augustine, *Confessions*, I, i, I.

follow the immutable law of Karma or the law of the conservation of moral energy, associated with the physical body, emotional mind and rational intellect of the soul.

It is important that the soul not be confused with its rational and biological sheaths, for the biological sheaths of the soul are more changeable and destructible than the intellectual ones. The soul in its pure form is a core, unaffected by mental, biological, and physical changes, but rational choice in man is important and powerful in the soul's journey through these changing planes. The life or immortality of the soul has been called *Manomaya Prana*, or psychic vitality, which Edgar Cayce referred to as Mind, the builder. The *Gita* says,

That Being, which is the ground of the entire existence is indestructible. No one is capable of destroying that invisible force. The bodies, which this eternal Soul puts on, are terminable; but the Soul itself is imperishable and external. . . . A person, who considers the Soul (pure self) to be the killer and the one who considers it to have been killed, both are ignorant, because the soul neither kills nor is it killed. The soul is neither born nor does it die in time; it does not come into being nor has it any future time to become again (immortality is above past, present and future; it is an eternal continuum). It is unborn, permanent, ever existent, ancient and is not destroyed in the perishable body. . . . Just as a man puts on new dress after casting off the old one, similarly the soul puts on a new body after laying aside the old one. Neither weapons can cut it; nor can fire burn it; nor water can moisten it; nor can the air dry it up. It is immune to cuts, burns, wetness, and dryness; it is ever existent, all sided, stable, and staionary. It is invisible, unthinkable and is incorruptible in itself.[2]

We note how close Edgar Cayce comes to these ideas about the nature of soul. Just as the philosophy of the *Gita*, based on the experiences of the great sages, tells us that the invisible ground of the entire cosmos is indestructible and the individual soul shares that indestructibility, so does Edgar Cayce. In one reading he says:

For we are joint heirs with that universal force we call God—if we seek to do His biddings. If our purposes are not in keeping with that Creative

[2] *Bhagavad-Gita*, II–17–20 and 21–24.

Force, or God, then we may be a hindrance. And, as it has been indicated of old, it has not appeared nor even entered into the heart of man to know the glories the Father has prepared for those that love Him. Neither may man conceive of destruction, even though he is in the earth a three–dimensional awareness. Neither may he conceive of horror, nor of suffering, nor even of what it means to be in outer darkness where the worm dieth not (5755–2).

Edgar Cayce had never read Sanskrit, never studied Hindu philosophy, and was philosophically rooted in his intensive study of the Bible. Moreover, the questions, which were posed by believers in Christianity, were within the context of that religion. His statements therefore, presumably clarify the metaphysical bases of the Christian philosophy. The breadth of the outlook in the readings simply mirrors the inherent universality of the Christian metaphysics. Jesus Christ had stated that the clarification of concepts would come through the spirit of truth, one and eternal. The theory of reincarnation and the immortality of the soul, as indicated in the philosophy of the *Gita*, is rooted in the concept of one immanent as well as transcendent Being, Universal Force or God, designated as Brahman in the Upanishads. The Upanishads, which predate the *Gita*, are the philosophic knowledge of the sages, attained through yoga, the unique communion with the Universal Force. The first manifestation of the unmanifest Brahman, mentioned in the Upanishads, is *Shabda Brahman* or word-God (Logos), the next being the light. Here we see the closeness of the Cayce readings to the ancient philosophy of India, as he interpreted the Christian philosophy, quoting the Gospel itself. In the same reading concerning the nature of the individual soul in relation to God, Cayce says, "Then in considering those conditions . . . those experiences as may be a part of the soul's awareness—in the beginning was the Word, and the Word was God and the Word was with God" (5753–2, p. 2).

Why does Edgar Cayce refer to God, the universal, all pervasive Cosmic Being? In hundreds of Cayce readings, we find that he immediately connects individual suffering with the soul and the soul to God. Later we shall see how he suggests that the remedy of that suffering is the love of God—man's consciousness of being an instrument of the Creative Force. Soul or self, as the image of God, is the key to the understanding of God, as the source of all existence. "The kingdom of God," which lies within the human personality in the form of the individuated soul, has separated from its Source, God, and is continuously striving to return to Him. The awareness of the relationship between the soul and God, through the practice of the positive attitude of love, appears to be the sum and substance of the Cayce readings. However, can we actually establish the existence of the individuated soul, and what is the significance of reincarnation? Quotations from the original sources of Hindu philosophy may establish how the basic ideas in the Cayce material are identical with the findings of the ancient sages.

The *Chandogya Upanishad* of 1200 B.C., while expounding the need of knowing the Self, the essence of human personality, states, "The Self, which is free from evil [not bodily self, but soul, the image of God in man], ageless, deathless, sorrowless, hungerless, thirstless, whose desire is The Real [longing for God], whose conception is the Real—He should be reached out, Him one should desire to understand. He obtains all worlds and all desires who has found out and who understands that Self."[3] Only the discovery of the divine element, the realization of the spiritual essence in one's self and in others, can make an individual rise from selfish desires to universal love. This realization itself is indicative of growth and development of human personality. When a man reaches that stage, he spontaneously behaves positively, renouncing hatred, jealousy, and selfishness. All of which brings him peace and tranquility, self-healing power and harmony, making him immune to all sufferings. The attainment of this state of existence is the ultimate goal of all individuals, because every man is potentially that great Self-Christ, which has been called *Atman* in Hinduism. Soul as a potentially transcendent entity, su-

[3] *Chandogya Upanishad*, VIII–VII–I.

perior to all spatiotemporal objects of the material world, is described in the Upanishads in the following passage:

He who consists of mind, whose body is life [Prana], whose form is light, whose conception is truth, whose self is space, containing all words, containing all desires, containing all odors, containing all tastes, encompassing the whole world, the unspeaking, the unconceived—this self of mine within the heart is smaller than a grain of rice or a barley corn, or a mustard seed, or a grain of a millet, or the kernel of a grain of millet; this self of mine within the heart is greater than the earth, greater than the atmosphere, greater than the sky, greater than these worlds. Containing all words, containing all desires, containing all odors, containing all tastes, encompassing the whole world, the unspeaking, the unconceived—this is the self of mine within the heart, this is Brahman. Into Him I shall enter on departing hence.[4]

The individual self, although subject to the law of reincarnation, the law of Karma, and finally the law of Grace, is in its true nature, the very kernel of kernels, invisible spirit. The sage of the Upanishads, quoted above, has attained the highest development of his self and has cancelled all his past accumulations of Karma through the law of Grace. Therefore, he is ready to embrace God. The embodied self, because of its intimate relation to God, is potentially divine and religion is the spiritual discipline which reunites it with God.

Edgar Cayce appears to have described this attitude of self-realization or *Moksha*—liberation from the cycle of physical births and deaths—in these words: "When opportunities are presented, it is entity's own will force that must be exercised. Then in every contact with others, there is the opportunity for a soul to fulfill in itself the Creative Forces from the First Cause, and to embrace that which is necessary for the entity to enter into at-oneness with the Creative Force" (5753). The last words "to enter into at-oneness with the Creative Force," are significant because they paraphrase the Upanishadic words, "This is the self of mine within the heart, this is Brahman [Creative Force]. Into Him I shall enter on departing hence." The sage who uttered these words had passed through vari-

[4]Ibid., VIII–VII–II.

ous levels of existence in his past lives and was ready to take the final step, having utilized all opportunities "to fulfill in itself the Creative Forces from the First Cause," as Edgar Cayce has put it. This relationship of the individual soul with God is important for understanding the theory of reincarnation.

What I call soul, *Jivatman*, or the individuated self, Edgar Cayce calls "entity," an appropriate term because the individual with whom he was concerned in the readings was the embodied soul. Even though his readings were chiefly concerned with the diagnosis of physical ailments, he laid more emphasis on the metaphysical self, the soul which had accumulated mental, intellectual, and even physical, Karmic traces. The physical body, occupied by the soul, is itself a combination of atoms and electrons influenced by the soul force. In Hinduism, the all-pervasive soul force (the electromagnetic-gravitational energy or its author), is also the effect of the universal Creative Force called Brahman. And so, the individual subject, or entity, emanating from Brahman, binds itself in a particular physical body according to the *Sanskaras*, the Karmic traces. Soul and body collaborate with each other because both have the same ultimate base, one being the subjective and the other being the objective and extended emanation from the same creative impulse.

The subjective emanation, the soul-entity, has the advantage of being the conscious perceiver, reasoning and thinking, while the body does not. Above all, the soul unlike the body, is self-conscious, i.e., it is aware of its own existence.

In other words, soul is neither body, nor mind, nor intellect, though it uses these aspects of personality as instruments of expression. The modern intellectual is justifiably dissatisfied with the lack of empirical evidence for the existence of the soul, particularly in the organized Christian church, where the existence of the soul is accepted on faith, and intellectual analysis of this term is rarely considered necessary. However, some secular philosophers have unwittingly contributed to the vague use of the terms *soul*, *God*, and *immortality*, saying that these are matters of faith and their acceptance or rejection is a matter of personal taste. Thus, religion is reduced to personal predilection, having little to do with objective truth, a tendency which has led to the impracticable compartmentalism of religion, philosophy, and science.

Here we begin to see the value of the guidance of the Indian sages, who have not accepted "soul" as a dogma, but as a fact. For them it is not a mere belief, but a reality; not an imaginary phantom, but an existent entity. If the soul is unobservable by. today's known instruments, so is the atom and the electron. The subtlety of a fact should not deter a scientist from recognizing it as reality, if its effects are clearly determined.

Philosophy and religion have never been segregated in Hindu culture but have collaborated in demonstrating empirical evidence for the existence of soul. Thousands of years of experimenting by Indian sages with the reality of the soul and the soul force resulted in the philosophy of the Vedas, the Upanishads and the *Bhagavad-Gita,* which present the philosophical theories of reincarnation and Karma. The theory of reincarnation, of the evolution of the soul, called *Punarjarma* (rebirth) in Hinduism, is a well-grounded theory, based on facts of observation and investigative method. It is intimately related to the doctrine of Karma, which propounds the law of the conservation of ethical energy and moral causation.

What is the empirical evidence for the existence of the soul, as something beyond body, beyond mind and beyond intellect? Without such evidence, any theory of the immortality of the soul, including the theory of reincarnation, must crumble. We have already postulated that the soul is the awareness or the subject of all experiences, and, as such, is self-evident. For there can be no knowledge without the knower, no thinking without the thinker and, in short, no experience without the experiencer or agent. This empirical evidence of the soul as subject, is so strong and unavoidable that rational rejection is impossible. No one can ever conceive the possibility of a situation where the knowledge and the known could ever be present without the knower, or the feeling and the object felt could be present without the subject, who experiences the feeling.

The Upanishads have therefore explained that the *Atman*, or the soul, is the source of all objective knowledge and experience. Descartes, the French philosopher, explains the same fact by adopting the method of doubt. He has stated that if we apply the method to everything that we experience, we shall ultimately reach a point where our doubt ends. Let me suppose that colors, which I see, are not actually colors. They only appear to be colors to my eyes; in reality they are different waves of light. So let me doubt the existence of colors. I may even doubt logic and scientific principles, because they are not always the source of valid knowledge, I may doubt the existence of the physical world, including the categories of time, space, figure, extension, and motion. I may come to believe that nothing is certain in this world. Even then I must be certain of one thing during this application of doubt. That one thing is the act of my doubting. I cannot deny the existence of this act. This very act of doubting, which is certain and indubitable, leads me to believe that I, as the doubter, do exist. If there were no doubter, the act would be nonexistent.

Doubting is thinking, which implies a thinker. That is why Descartes accepted the existence of the self, the doubter, the thinker, or the perceiver, as a self-evident truth. He expressed this proposition by saying "*Cogito ergo sum*—I think, therefore I exist." Though this unquestionable knowledge of the self or soul has been called intuitive, yet it is empirical and logically consistent. The reader himself, in passing through the stages of doubt, from the extreme of regarding the whole world as uncertain, to the absolute certainty of the existence of the self as doubter, can personally experience this evidence.

Even the great skeptical philosopher, David Hume, could not really succeed in demolishing the self-evidence of the existence of the human experience. He said, "When I come across the problem of what I am, I always think of some activity or other. I identify my existence with the experiences of seeing, hearing, touching, smelling, tasting, imagining, dreaming. When I take away seeing, hearing, tasting, smelling, touching, imagining, I find that I don't exist." It is worth noting that Hume, while denying the existence of his own self, cannot get rid of the pronoun *I*. Thus, his conclusion, "I find that I don't exist," is logically invalid and self-contradictory. He acts like a man, who leaving his own office after working for several hours, peeps through the window and reports, "Look, I am not there. I don't exist." How can it be possible for a man to go out of the room and also be in the room, unless he could split himself into two identical personalities? Certainly Descartes scored a victory over Hume in this controversy, with his irrefutable exercise of the self.

Hindu philosophy goes a step further. It strengthens the indubitableness of the soul by offering psychological evidence, acceptable even to contemporary psychology, for the existence of a deeper aspect of human personality. Modern psychology and its branches have gradually been moving toward a concept of the soul, or the psyche, which recognizes that the self possesses potentialities which are yet unknown and unfathomed. Parapsychology, the latest branch of psychology, is still in its embryonic stage. But the ancient Hindu sages had discovered these powers of the psyche and even brought these potential forces to the level of consciousness from the depths of the unconscious self.

The sages of India, having experienced the existence of the soul in their own being, shared their knowledge with their pupils. They could arrive at intelligible concepts, which could be accepted as the empirical basis of the soul's existence. However, the fact remains that the soul, although an existent phenomenon in conscious experience, must always be the knower, never the known; always the perceiver, but never the thing perceived. However, no known fact and no perceived thing can ever be apprehended without its presence. That is why the Upanishads say that unseen, it sees; unheard, it hears; untouched, unsmelled, untasted, it experiences the senses. The discovery of the soul is a self-discovery. It is a consciousness, which does not need any outward object, but an inward gaze. In its essence the soul is something more than consciousness. Even when we are at the semiconscious or subconscious level of dreams, do we ever miss the presence of the self?

In all dreams we find ourselves present. Even in dreaming our own death, we find ourselves the experiencer. This continuous presence of the self in the dream state is evidence of the soul as experiencer, just as self-consciousness is its evidence at the waking level. Let us accept for a moment the argument of the skeptic that in the conscious state we only conventionally label the experiences of seeing, hearing, and otherwise sensing, as the experiences of a subject. We use the pronoun "I" as a convention, whereas in reality the self does not exist. But consider the dream state, certainly nonconventional. Psychologists claim that dreams are frequently the opposite of our consciously motivated actions. But in spite of this antagonism between waking and dreaming, the continuity of the subject is not lost, thus confirming the transcendental nature of the soul.

The soul transcends the experiences of the senses, because it is always the subject standing above the objects apprehended, above the experience. In the triad of knower, known, and knowledge, it is the knower that stands above the other two. Hence, the knower is called transcendent. Similarly, in the dream state, the knower-self is ever present and ever experiencing. Now let us consider what happens to consciousness and subconsciousness when we are in deep sleep, below even the dream state.

There is no consciousness, no sense perception, no imagining, or even dreaming. We are in virtual death so far as the experiences of the subjective self are concerned. But upon awaking from this sleep, we may say, "Oh, I enjoyed such a sound sleep." Does this not empirically indicate that in spite of the discontinuity, the self, as the agent, has continued to exist?

Beyond the stage of deep sleep is the state called *Turiya*, the transcendental soul existence. In this state the conscious, the subconscious, and deep-sleep levels are transcended. This does not imply annihilation of the other levels, but rather, it means amalgamation of the other three, into one continuity—one wholeness. The *Turiya* state, which is obtained by yoga, is the fourth dimension of the mind, which rises above the relativity of the three dimensions of human experience mentioned above.

The *Turiya* state is the finding of the Hindu sages. Later we shall explain the method of yoga, but it is sufficient to state here that yoga is the empirical method of experiencing the existence of the soul as a transcendent entity. At the highest level gained through yoga, the knowledge, the knower and the known, consciousness, dream consciousness, and deep sleep, are all merged into one continuous experience. Seventy-five years ago this theory of the invisible soul might well have been doubted. Its immeasurable potentialities of rising above space and time would have been ridiculed. But it is not the case today.

Nineteenth-century science had been obsessed by the theory of mechanical causation. It had regarded all the phenomena of nature, including life and mind, subject to determinism; they could all be explained by the mechanical laws of cause and effect. But researches in the field of physics during the early part of the twentieth century have reversed the situation. They have forced the scientists to accept the existence of a spiritual force or a cosmic psyche, which appears to be behind all motion, behind all evolution and dynamic development of the cosmos.

The two theories of physics, which have revolutionized science and shaken the gross materialism of the nineteenth century are the quantum theory and the theory of relativity. The quantum theory, propounded by Max Planck, concerns the radiation of bodies when heated. It shows that when bodies are heated, radiant energy is emitted in discontinous bits called quanta, where previously it had been believed that in radiation, energy flowed continuously.

It is a matter of common experience that when any heated body becomes extremely brilliant from intense heat, with the gradual increase of temperature, it first gives a red glow, which changes successively to orange, yellow, and white.

Planck's problem was to develop a mathematical equation to explain this phenomenon. He had to find out how the qualitative change of the colors of the heated bodies could be explained quantitatively. This explanation could establish how the amount of radiant energy so emitted is related to wave length and temperature.

Mathematical calculation has helped the physicists to determine the wave length of all visible and invisible radiation in the electromagnetic spectrum. The visible spectrum runs from that of red light at .00007 centimeter to violet at .00004 centimeter. Just below the limits of the human eye are the ultraviolet rays which may be recorded on photographic film and similarly, immediately beyond the limits at the other end are the infrared rays, experienced by our skin as heat. Besides the ultraviolet rays, physicists have discovered that there are Xrays, gamma rays, radio waves, and cosmic rays, which are electromagnetic, and not observable by the human eye.

Planck invented an equation to explain the phenomenon of quanta which successfully explained the radiation color changes, but what is the significance of the theory? First, it shows that there is a harmony in the qualitative change or color and the quantitative amount of energy. Secondly, it suggests that light consists of discontinuous particles. Einstein called these particles, or grains of energy, photons. This theory of light comes in direct conflict with the other theory, according to which light consists of waves. Many phenomena of light strongly confirm that light does not consist of individual particles or corpuscles, but is a continuous flow of waves. Yet the photoelectric law of Einstein, which holds good in a vast range of the phenomena of radiation, clearly proves that light consists of particles. The net result of these researches is that a dualistic explanation of light has been accepted. Light is both particles and waves. Similar research in the structure of the atom has disproved the idea that an electron has always a definite position in space. The behavior of an electron is capricious and too complex to be measured accurately. Thus, a dualistic view of the nature of electrons holds that electrons, like light, behave sometimes as waves and sometimes as particles. The scientists, therefore, have come to the conclusion that it is meaningless for a physicist to attempt to determine the exact nature of electrons or of light. But at the same time, the success of the mathematical conclusions continues to point toward a harmonious one. The presence of a psychic or spiritual force beyond human calculation is being confirmed each day by science.

Einstein, the unique scientific genius of our century, had a firm belief that the universe is not the result of a chance combination of blind forces, but a uniform system, which is being propelled by an intelligent Force. He has confirmed this view by showing that time and space are relative. His postulates have been tried, both with regard to nuclear energy in the atom and to discoveries in recent space travel. The behavior of the galaxies and interstellar systems is uniform, though not mechanical. So is the case with the behavior of the smallest bit of matter, the electron. Man stands midway between the electron and the universe. Hence the secret of the nature and behavior of creation lies within the nature of man, who is both a spiritual being and a material structure.

A significant fact is that the mathematical calculations, which are the product of the human mind hold good in explaining phenomena which are not visible to the human eye and yet are verifiable. This attests that the human psyche is not only more than physical, but also more than the intellectual or rational element, more than consciousness. The structure of the soul is invisible, yet verifiable like the structure of the electron or of radiation.

Hence the concept of soul as an invisible, activating, psychic force, which is the directive, unitive, subjective center of human personality and the subtlest basis even of the subtle intellect, is not unscientific. The fact remains that most religions have taken the concept of soul for granted and have not experimented with its nature, as Hinduism has. In the absence of such experimentation and with little concern for the nature of soul, a religion tends to become a blind faith and a ridicule of science and philosophy. A third possibility is that without the knowledge and experience of the nature of soul, religion may be accepted as an appendage, having practical social utility. The spirit of religion is neglected and the forms and ceremonials are magnified. Religion is not an inner experience of the soul, but an ostentation of a dogma. Its profession is a matter of convenience in day-to-day life. This is what appears to have happened today to religion the world over. Having been conditioned by such a religious atmosphere the average man is steeped in utter darkness with regard to the soul.

To the Vedic sages the soul was *Atman*, literally the center or nucleus. As the center or nucleus of human personality, *Atman* is individuated spirit, Brahman—Mind, and Source of everything that has being. This Cosmic Consciousness or Psyche is immanent in the spatiotemporal world and yet is more than the cosmic existence.

The soul is an entity which is noncorporeal, but individuated, and, which, when embodied, is the nucleus of the rational, mental, and physical aspects of human personality. This subtlest aspect of man's total intellectual, mental, and physical constitution, is not mere consciousness, but something more. On the one hand, this individuated spirit or soul has contact with the spatiotemporal world, through sensuous experiences and, on the other hand, it has contact with the spiritual realm, beyond time, space, and causality. Its contact with the external world is through the mediacy of intellect, mind, and body. Thus an embodied soul or man is an integrated whole of body, mind, intellect, and soul.

So we see man as a miniature universe or the image of God in the sense that his functions parallel God's manifestation in the form of the cosmic center, the galactic center, the center of the solar system, the moon and the earth. The core of man's personality controls the periphery of his intellect and body, and it is this soul center in man which comes into contact with the Universal Mind. However, just as a radio, which is switched off, cannot relay the music in the air, similarly, the soul of man cannot transcend the earthly limitations of time and space if it is not attuned, through spiritual discipline, to the Cosmic Consciousness. Thus, the soul, itself independent of the intellect, mind and body, is greater than the sum of these, and is their very activator. In describing the subtle nature of the soul, the *Gita* says, "The senses are subtler than the body, the mind is subtler than the senses; subtler than the mind is the intellect, and subtler than the intellect is the soul."

Thus we see in this hierarchy that the gross dimension depends upon and is controlled by the subtler one. The functions of the body, including those of the senses, are apprehended and controlled by mind. The urges of mind are controlled by rational dimension of the self and that in turn is the offshoot of the soul which controls as well the subconscious and unconscious dynamism of man.

We have already seen the empirical evidence of this unitive function of the soul. As long as a person identifies himself with body, mind, intellect, and even ego, he does not reach the core of his being. The soul is greater than, and the background of, the ego itself. The sole purpose of religion is to bring about the realization of this transcendental soul. It is through the understanding and the utilization of his spiritual potentialities that the individual rises above the antinomies, contradictions, and relativities of pleasure and pain, loss and gain, heat and cold, praise and blame.

When a man comes to realize that his true soul-self is neither body, nor mind, nor rationality, nor ego, but something more and the very ground of all these, a flash of inner light expands his attitude and he is not disturbed by the relativities and the distracting disabilities of ordinary existence. He sees the unity in diversity and the harmony in discord. He recognizes the light of God in his contact with persons who differ from him, and then alone can he understand what is meant by the commandment, "Love thy neighbor as thyself." In his day-to-day behavior with family, friends, and neighbors, with young and old, with superiors and inferiors, he continuously maintains an attitude of love, reverence and identity, in spite of the apparent differences. It is only then that he has reached the stage of self-realization, knowing that the soul, which is the emanation from God, is in constant connection with God.

This connection remains dormant as long as man identifies himself only with the body, mind, and ego. To activate the contact, a selfless attitude of service and love has been advocated in all true religions and reaffirmed by Edgar Cayce in the same spirit. In one of the Cayce readings, he says, "Life in self then is God. . . . For as ye do it unto others ye are doing it to the God in YOURSELF! Thus you are by example as well as precept making for the true relationships to Creative Forces that may aid thee from without to the influence or force of God WITHIN self" (1436–3, p. 3).

It is essential to raise the question of why the immortal, incorruptible, spiritual soul takes on the physical body. Why should it be emphasized by Edgar Cayce in all his readings that men must practice love and not hatred, tolerance and not impatience, in order to bring back the primeval glory of the soul? Once again we may ask why it is that in all the readings, Edgar Cayce again and again returns to the relationship of the soul, the entity, with God. Why does he go on repeating ceaselessly that man should take care of his relationship with God under all circumstances?

Let me give some concrete examples from some of the readings. While answering a question of a lady of twenty-seven years about her attitude toward her father, mother, and brother, Cayce says, "Who is thy father, who is thy mother? They that do the things necessary in thy experience that ye may learn, that ye may know, thy HEAVENLY Father the better.

"These are thy material parents. Then aid THEM in seeing; NOT by preaching, NOT by mere precept, but by LIVING a normal, balanced, Godly life among them!" (1436–3, p. 3).

While talking about different nations and heads of nations, Cayce insists upon the relationship of the soul with God. He states, "Just as one may see illustrated in conditions existent in the earth today. Each nation, each individual head of a nation, is not in the position it occupies merely by a 'happen chance' but by the grace of God. Thus it is needful for man to interpret in his own experience, 'the Lord thy God is one' " (5142–2, p. 1).

Cayce constantly reminds man that the sole purpose of life is to unite with God, the Creative Force. He does so in nearly all his readings, whether they are concerned with health, heredity, or environment. Talking about the influence of environment, he says:

Environs and hereditary influences are much deeper than that which is ordinarily conceded in the psychology of the present day. For the environs and the hereditary influences are spiritual as well as physical, and are physical because of the spiritual application of the abilities of the entity in relationship to spiritual development. For the purpose of each soul's experience in the earth is to become one with the Creative Forces that manifest in human experience, if it [the soul] will but *apply* same in its relationships to its fellow man. Hence what one is today is because of what . . . (the individual soul) *has done about that,* [it], knows *of* the Creative Force or God.   852–12, p. 1

Whether the problem is physical or material, domestic or social, personal or impersonal, Edgar Cayce always emphasizes that no one should forget that man's presence as an embodied soul on the planet has a purpose, and that purpose may be summed up as the realization of the relationship of the individual soul with God. I conclude the discussion of Soul by quoting Edgar Cayce, stating in clear-cut terms that the whole human personality, body and mind, is the manifestation of God: "Know that thy body, thy mind, thy soul, is a manifestation of God in the earth—as is every other soul; and that thy body is indeed the temple of the living God. All the good, then, all the God . . . that ye may know, is manifested in and through thyself—and not what somebody else thinks, not what somebody else does!" (2970–1, p. 2).

Cayce is perhaps the first Westerner who has made an attempt to clarify the concept of soul and its relationship to God in the manner of the highly developed philosophy of ancient India—the philosophy of the Upanishads and the *Bhagavad-Gita.* His ideas are not theoretically arrived at through discursive reasoning, but are the outcome of a real spiritual experience of oneness with the Cosmic Consciousness, during the *Turiya* state. Like the sages of ancient India and the yogins of all times, Edgar Cayce fulfilled the conditions of spiritual experiment, in which the effects of the existence of the soul as the subtle entity are demonstrated in the physical laboratory. This experience of Edgar Cayce, recorded in thousands of files, is empirical evidence of the existence of the soul, as the Center of all centers, Truth of all truths, and as the core of human personality.

Why does this invisible potentiality, Divine Soul, bind itself to the spatiotemporal world? In order to answer this question it is essential to explain the theory and purpose of reincarnation and the doctrine of Karma.

6 ॐ

The Nature and Purpose of Reincarnation

The doctrine of Karma and the theory of reincarnation are the two pillars of Hindu philosophy, in which are included Buddhism, Jainism, and Sikhism. Hinduism should not be confused with other instituted religions with dogmatic principles and rituals, for it is more accurately a philosophical and cultural system. Its cultural background dates to the time of the Vedas, the most ancient philosophic literature available in the world today. The term Veda literally means science or systematized knowledge, and is derived from the root *vid*, to know, from which the English word *wit* also derived.

The antiquity of the Vedic literature does not indicate a primitive level of beliefs, for the Vedas, as we have seen in the case of the scientific theory of the universe, have a profound, consistent philosophy, science, and religion. Notably, the remoteness of the Vedas gives testimony to the truth of Edgar Cayce's description of the highly advanced scientific culture of the Atlanteans, frequently believed to be impossible in the light of accepted theories of cultural evolution.

The Vedic literature was preserved by word of mouth for thousands of years before it was reduced to writing, thereby confusing historians attempting to decipher correct meanings. A great injustice has been done to research in the Vedic culture by European scholars, who were the first to translate and to interpret the literature to the

Western world, during the eighteenth and nineteenth centuries. They were handicapped, first because they were foreigners, without a grasp of the Vedic language in its true spirit, and secondly, because they tried to read their own historical theories into the Vedas. That is why they distorted the meanings of many terms to suit their prejudices, depicting the scientific culture as primitive animism and polytheism. Actually, the Vedas are a storehouse of theories about the nature of the cosmos, its evolution as well as the evolution of that miniature cosmos, man. The Vedas have no mythology, but cosmology; no theology, but metaphysics, which borders on astrophysics and astronomy, as we will see more clearly in studying the nature of God and theory of Divine Descent or the *Avataravada*. The *Mantras*, one portion of the Vedic literature, which have been wrongly labeled as hymns by Western scholars, are the statements of the constitution and function of the universe. The scientific nature of the writings, which may date back to 2500 B.C., is baffling. Although European scholars have misrepresented the culture by distorting its chronology, recent archeological evidence from the Indus Valley civilization supports its claim to antiquity.

The dynamic quality of the philosophy is indicated even in the language, by the fact that all nouns in the Vedic literature are rooted in verbs. The very names of the *Devatas* (wrongly translated as gods) are the names of the cosmic forces associated with the Creative Energy, first manifestation of the Unmanifest God. As an example, let us analyze the Sanskrit term *Hridayam* (heart).

This term, *Hridayam*, has been selected purposely, because it stands both for the central physiological organ in the human body, and also for the Central Energy of the cosmos. It is a combination of the three roots *hri-da-yam*. The verbal root *hri*, means taking in; *da* means giving out, and *yam* means controlling or balancing. Thus *Hridayam* is that which takes in, gives out and controls. The *Hridayam* or heart as the physiological organ of the human body has the threefold function of pumping in, pumping out, and controlling the circulation of blood. The term used for the Central Energy, the cosmic force, is *Hrichhakti* which is the sum of the threefold motion designated by the word *Hridayam*. In this context *hri* means inward motion; *da* means outward motion, and *yam* means the meeting point of inward and outward motion. This threefold pulsation of the Cosmic Energy explains the entire process of creation, evolution, and destruction of the physical universe bound by space, time, and causality. The inward motion is called *agati*, which pervades the whole universe. It is due to this inward motion that the whole cosmos is evolving and growing. This function is the manifestation of the Vishnu or preserving aspect of God, as the Supreme Person. It is the Christ aspect, associated with love, which motivates the function of preservation. That is why *Vishnu Devata* has been designated as the preserver.

The outward motion is called *gati*. It represents the function of destruction and is the manifestation of the *Shiva* (Holy Ghost), or destructive aspect of God as the Supreme Person, designated as *Shiva Devata*, the destroyer. Destruction here means annihilation of physical matter or the material body of man for the realization of the spiritual or divine self. The conjunction of the inward and outward motion has been called *sthiti*, stability. It represents the function of creation or origination of all the living and nonliving beings. This function is the manifestation of the Brahma (Father) or creative aspect of God as the Supreme Person, designated as *Brahma Devata*, the creator.

This threefold motion is the totality of the Creative Energy of the Supreme Person, not in the sense of human personality, but in the sense of cosmic, invisible, omniscient, omnipresent, omnipotent, and unchanging ground of the changing world of time, space, and causality. This totality is summed up in the English word, God.

Param Purusha, or literally, Supreme Person, Himself is unaffected by these three forces of His own Creative Energy. Just as the self in human personality remains the same identifiable entity, in spite of the changes of the physical body, of the mental feelings and of the intellectual ideas, similarly the Cosmic Self, the Supreme Person, remains unaffected by the changes in the world. Supreme Person in this sense is the real Unmoved Mover, because He is the cause of the threefold motion and yet is not affected by that motion. In a broad sense, this activity is the expression of His will, and is called *Leela*, the Play. Edgar Cayce has referred to this will or play of God as His desire to create individual souls to be the companions of the Supreme Person. In the words of Edgar Cayce, the answer to the question, "What is the purpose of the entry of a soul into material manifestations?" is "In the beginnings, or in the activities in which the soul manifested individually, it was for the purpose of becoming as a companion of Creative Force or God." (1650–1).

This statement of Edgar Cayce becomes intelligible when we refer to the notion of the Supreme Person and also to the Play in the form of the manifestation of His Creative Energy, *Maya* or *Prakriti*. This Energy has, on the one hand, brought about the universe of time, space and causality, and on the other, created the individuated souls or selves. Edgar Cayce referred to this Energy in his words, "Each soul that enters, then, must have had an impetus from some beginning that is of the Creative Energy, or of a first cause. . . . Hence, every form of life that man sees in a material world is an essence or manifestation of the Creator; not the Creator, but a manifestation of a first cause—and in its own sphere, its own consciousness of its activity in that plane or sphere" (5753–1).

Significantly, this quotation is a paraphrase of the philosophy of Hinduism, which distinguishes between *Purusha* as the Creator, and His Creative Energy, *Maya* or *Prakriti*. Both the objective beings, from the physical elements to animals, and the subjective human soul, are called nature. In other words, the physical creatures, living and nonliving, up to the level of animals, form one part of nature, and human souls form the other part. God, as Creator, has created both through His *Maya*.

When Cayce refers to "Creative Force or God," he includes both God as Supreme Person and as *Maya*. A clarification from the Vedic literature will help to define these terms, and to put them in their proper place.

The Vedic philosophy consists of a vast literature, including the

Mantras, mentioned before; *Brahmanas*, which are the explanatory comments on the *Mantras;* the *Upanishads*, which are the philosophical conclusions concerning the Vedic researches; and *Bhagavad-Gita*, the quintessence of Hinduism uttered by Lord Krishna to his disciple, Arjuna. According to the Vedic philosophy, the creation of the universe is divided into three categories: the macrocosmic, interstellar cosmos, representing the world Soul; the individuated souls or human beings; and the microcosmic elements which also constitute the physical bodies of animals and men.

The infinite, invisible Pure Spirit is the one transcendental source of all existence, assuming the form of Ishwara, God, the omnipotent and indestructible Self, as the unchangeable ground of the changing cosmos. Another reading of Edgar Cayce is almost a paraphrase of the Vedic theory of creation, historically at least 4000 years prior to his birth. He raises the question of the relationship of the soul with matter on the one hand and God on the other, clearly stating that the microcosmic material creation is related to the First Cause, as is man. He says, "Hence in the various spheres that man sees (that are demonstrated, manifested, in and before self) even in a material world, all forces, all activities, are a manifestation. Then, that which would be the companionable, the at-oneness with, the ability to be one with, becomes necessary for the demonstration or manifestation of those attributes in and through all force, all demonstration, in a sphere" (5753–1).

That man stands between the material forces on the one hand, and the spiritual manifestation of God on the other, is further supported in the same reading which states:

Because an atom, a matter, a form, is changed does not mean that the essence, the source or the spirit of it has changed; only in its form of manifestation, and *not* in its relation with the first cause. That man reaches that consciousness in the material plane of being aware of what he does about or with the consciousness of the knowledge, the intelligence . . . produces that which is known as the entering into the first cause, principles, basis, or the essence, that there may be demonstrated in that manifested that which gains for the soul, for the entity, that which would make the soul an accept-able companion to the Creative Force, Creative Influence.   5753–1, p. 2

Completing a paraphrase of the Vedic philosophy of threefold creation, the Edgar Cayce reading continues:

In the beginning was that which set in motion that which is seen in manifested form with the laws governing same. The inability of destroying matter, the ability of each force, each source of power or contact—as it meets in its various forms, produces that which is a manifestation in a particular sphere. This may be seen in those elements used in the various manifested ways of preparing for man, in many ways, those things that bespeak of the laws that govern man's relationship to the first cause, or God.   5753–1, p. 2

In the three Vedic categories of creation in which man is flanked by the First Cause as the world soul, and the First Cause as material manifestation, let us clarify the relationship of God, man, and the world. As stated, all three categories of creation rest on God, the Unmoved Mover, *Purusha*, which in this context may be translated as Self, the noncorporeal aspect of First Cause. *Prakriti*, which may be translated as nature, is the dynamic corporeal force which brings about the manifestation of all three categories of material creation.

Arising out of the incorporeal force of the *Purusha* is *Ishwara*, the soul of the macrocosmic aspect of creation. While the individual cosmic and galactic centers themselves may be destroyed, *Ishwara* is noncorporeal and indestructible. Similarly, the soul forces, or *Deva-tas*, controlling individual centers, are indestructible. *Ishwara* is the motionless ground beyond all corporeal phenomena, on which the constant motion of the macrocosmic aspect of the Divine Creation is dependent.

The fivefold division of human life, corresponds to the fivefold classification of the *Devatas* of earth, moon, sun, galactic and cosmic centers. The physical body of man represents the earth; the mind, the moon; the intellect, the sun. The impersonal unconscious of the self represents the galactic center, and the pure self or noncorporeal spirit, the cosmic center. The cosmic center, or *Svayambhu Prajapati*, though destructible in its corporeal aspect, has the indestructible Self of pure spirit in it. In fact, that pure Spirit is all-pervasive and is rooted in every individuated thing, whether it be macrocosmic *Devata* or man or a physical microcosmic entity such as an electron. It is only the corporeal aspect of each entity, which is destructible. Edgar Cayce has expressed exactly the same opinion in one of the readings, when he says, "Because an atom, a matter, a form, is changed does not mean that the essence, the source or the spirit of it has changed; only in its form of manifestation, and *not* in its relation with the first cause" (5753–1). It is impressive that all Cayce readings concerning man, matter, and cosmos consistently use the term Spirit and First Cause in exactly the same sense as *Param Purusha* and *Svayambhu* have been used in the Vedic philosophy. In addition, his theory of creation would remain unintelligible to a layman without having recourse to the above explanation.

The second category of creation, the human institution, stands midway between the macrocosmic and the microcosmic categories. It has been called *Adhyatman,* or the category of soul, a combination of the infinite, incorporeal element of pure spirit, and the corporeal element of physical energy. It is this soul which takes birth in the form of a *Jiva,* a living human being, and is reincarnated. Edgar Cayce referred to *Jiva* as "the entity." Man is a miniature universe, the image of God in the sense that he resembles the Cosmic Person. His soul is the indestructible and infinite aspect. The physical, the mental or emotional, and the rational or intellectual aspects, are the destructible elements. However, during reincarnation, the mental tendencies, the intellectual tendencies as well as tendencies in the impersonal unconscious aspect of his personality continue with the human soul in the form of Karma. Many times even the physical tendencies are carried by the soul, in the form of Karma, from birth to birth. It is only when all the Karmas are exhausted that the pure self returns to God, the Supreme Person, the One.

The third category of creation, the microcosmic, is the *Adhibhutam* or material creation of the dynamic world. This category has five material elements as visible entities, corresponding to the fivefold aspects of the macrocosmic and human categories. The five corporeal elements are the earth element, or physical solid matter, corresponding to the planet earth; the moist element corresponding to the moon; the light element, corresponding to the sun; the air or gaseous element, corresponding to the galactic center; and the space or ether, corresponding to the cosmic center. Note that in the case of the material constitution, the space element or *Akasha,* is the indestructible center or base, just as in the case of human constitution, the soul is the center and in the macrocosmic constitution, the cosmic person is the indestructible element. The *Akashic* records (the records preserved in the indestructible aspect of the physical cosmos) referred to by Edgar Cayce, are the traces of the individual souls, who have been reincarnated in the world.

One God as Supreme Being, incorporating the threefold constitutions, can be represented in the following chart:

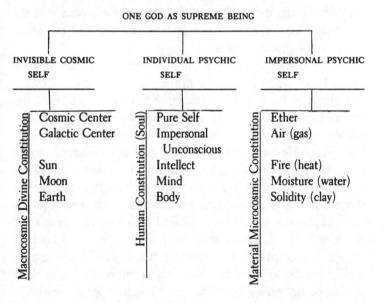

ONE GOD AS SUPREME BEING

INVISIBLE COSMIC SELF	INDIVIDUAL PSYCHIC SELF	IMPERSONAL PSYCHIC SELF
Cosmic Center	Pure Self	Ether
Galactic Center	Impersonal Unconscious	Air (gas)
Sun	Intellect	Fire (heat)
Moon	Mind	Moisture (water)
Earth	Body	Solidity (clay)

Macrocosmic Divine Constitution — Human Constitution (Soul) — Material Microcosmic Constitution

The Nature and Purpose of Reincarnation   81

We see here in this "genealogy" how the unmoved world Soul or Self manifests itself in cosmic motion as the cosmic center around which the universes in turn revolve. The entire motion of these bodies is grounded on this self-caused center, the stable base, source and cause, which is not motion itself. God as the ground of the entire motion, is therefore, the immanent cause of the cosmos. He is further visibly manifested in the galactic center as the Light of Lights and the Sun of Suns. This center, called *Parameshthi*, is also Vishnu, or the preserving aspect of God. It is the source of all solar energy, guiding the motion of the solar systems and is thus the cause of their preservation. We find in this the Christ aspect, which descends periodically to earth in divine incarnations. As Lord Krishna says in the *Bhagavad-Gita*, "I am Vishnu, the light of lights among the shining suns." And Jesus Christ also says, "As long as I am in this world, I am the light of the world." This source of light and energy is manifested sequentially in the sun, the source of energy for our solar system; the moon, whose orbit is under the guidance of the energy·and motion which emanate from the sun; and the earth, which revolves around the sun.

God, besides being immanent in the three constitutions of creation as Mind, is also beyond these three. As already stated, God has four planes of being. God as infinite, is beyond all attributes and exceeds even the state of Oneness. In the second state God is pure essence, pure consciousness. Even here He is beyond all personification, though He is the Subject, without any objective opposition. In one sense this is the Holy Ghost aspect of the transcendent nature of God, with the other two stages respectively representing the Father and Son. The fourth plane represents the immanent nature of God. This is the manifestation of God both as consciousness and power, soul or self, and creative energy. But even at this level He remains unaffected by time, space and causality, the spatiotemporal world being the effect of His spirit, which enters into the world as psychic energy, giving rise to the three constitutions of creation.

In the divine constitution God, the Father, is the Supreme Person. He is the Goal to be achieved. In the human constitution, man, the son, has both the infinite aspect of the divinity and the finitude of the body, mind, and intellect. His divine aspect is the soul whose goal is the self-realization of reaching the Divine Source. Man is the highest manifested form because he is both divine and visible self. He is self-conscious and this self-consciousness prompts him to rid himself of the material limitations and to return to God. In the words of Edgar Cayce, "What then is the purpose of the entity's activity in the consciousness of mind, matter, spirit in the present?

"That it, the entity, may *know* itself to *be* itself and part of the Whole; not the Whole but one *with* the Whole; and thus retaining its individuality, knowing itself to be itself yet one with the purposes of the First Cause that called it, the entity, into *being,* into the awareness, into the consciousness of itself.

"That is the purpose, that is the cause of *being*" (826–11, p. 2).

This statement of Edgar Cayce is an exact expression of what we have said about human constitution. The very purpose of the creation of man is self-realization. In man himself there is the trinity of soul, mind and body—Father, Son, and Holy Ghost.

There are three courses to self-realization or at-onement with God. The first is the *Karma Yoga* or the path of Karma, which is a gradual evolution of the soul toward God. When the method of moving toward the goal is material and the aim also is material, i.e., the attainment of the highest Creative Energy, the path is called *Karma Yoga.* Simply, even when a person does not bother about the worship of God and does not subject himself to a religious approach, he slowly continues to advance toward perfection through his Karmic action in thousands of reincarnations. His goal in this world is the attainment of the highest skill in his profession or occupation, which ultimately brings him into contact with the Creative Energy. But, by following this path of trial and error, he must both suffer and gain a great deal, as Edgar Cayce has mentioned in many life readings. However, with voluntary choice of benevolent actions, he can quicken his march to

God, rid himself of the cycle of reincarnations, and attain liberation.

The second path is the path of devotion or love called the *Bhakti Yoga*. In this path the goal is divine, but the method is worldly. The individual subordinates all his worldly material actions to the love of God. He worships Him as the Supreme Person, the Father and the Master, and follows the path of love in every human undertaking. Edgar Cayce lays more emphasis on this path in his life readings.

The third route is that of intuitive knowledge or the *Jnana Yoga*. Here both the goal and method are divine. Following this path, the individual attains divine knowledge through the inner approach of meditation, ultimately changing the natural empirical state of man into the divine nonnatural state. This is the real meaning of the statement of Jesus that a Christian must be born again.

Why have we stated that man as a self-conscious agent aspires to return to God, the Father? Edgar Cayce has reiterated in his readings that the glory of God is to be manifested in the entire creation. The following quotation indicates how materiality has been conceived by him as the way to God:

"Each entity enters materiality for a purpose. That all the experiences in the earth are as one is indicated by the desires, the longings, as arise within the experience of that which makes for the growing, the knowing within self—*Mind!* Thus does the entity, as a whole, become aware that it, itself, in body, mind, and soul, is the result—each day—of the application of laws pertaining to creation, this evolution, this soul-awareness within, consciously manifested" (1947-3, p. 4). When referred to the threefold creation, this becomes a clear statement of the purpose of man's emanation from, and return to, God. Cayce restates the basic truth expounded by the sages of India in the following: "What is the purpose of entering consciousness? That each phase of body, mind and soul may be to the glory of that Creative Force in which it moves and has its being" (1947-3, p. 4).

The expression "each phase" is worth noting. It appears that the sleeping sage Cayce was pointing to the three phases of creation—

material, which he calls body; human, which he calls mind; and divine, which he calls soul. Also note that he uses the words "glory of that Creative Force." That Creative Force, in which all phases of creation exist, is undoubtedly that aspect of God which is immanent in the cosmos. It is remarkable that, in spite of his lifelong study of the Bible and his orthodox Christian background, he was not prompted to use either "Christ" or "God" in the personal sense in this context. The explanation must be that, while giving life readings, he was in communion with the Universal Truth.

Reincarnation literally means the soul's continuous entry into human life and human consciousness on earth, interspersed with its existence in other forms and levels. Quitting the human body, according to the sages, it remains in a subtle body on the earth level for three days. On the fourth day it goes to the mental plane, corresponding to the lunar level. Normally the soul returns to this earth, born into a family and a situation in accord with its Karmas or action patterns of past birth. When a soul is reincarnated as a child it usually forgets all past experiences, but these experiences and acquired skills do remain dormant in the unconscious mind of the entity. The doctrine of Karma, which may be called the law of retribution or conservation of ethical energy, may be summed up in the statement, "As you sow, so shall you reap." As the law of the conservation of ethical energy, it explains the problem of evil and the differences of skills and talents among human beings.

Reincarnation should not be confused with transmigration of soul from man to bird or beast. Reincarnation means only that human soul is always incarnated as a human being, though it may sometimes change its sex. Because man is the most complete image of God, neither the Edgar Cayce readings nor Hindu philosophy teaches transmigration of souls to lower levels of being.

The individual soul has to work out its Karma, to make the right choice of ascending back to the divine level and ultimately experiencing at-onement with the Maker. The sole purpose of reincarnation of the individual soul is to destroy the accumulated Karmas, to empty the self of all the impediments to its self-luminosity. We shall see in a later chapter how this can be accomplished at a quicker pace. Our present concern is why all individual souls must pass through various incarnations. Every appearance of the entity affords it the opportunity to be awakened to the realization of God, by directing all thoughts to the understanding of God and His manifestations, all feelings to the love of God and His human manifestation. Karma is not an asset, but the impediment toward such realization. Certainly the law of Grace is higher than the law of Karma. Voluntary acceptance of Grace by attuning oneself to the Cosmic Consciousness in selfless action, divine love and deep understanding of the ideal, leads to the release of the soul from the relativity of Karma and reincarnation.

It is the prerogative of man alone to exercise this choice and to quicken his march toward God. It is the privilege of man and not of the animal or material nature, to work consciously for the reunion of the soul with its Maker. In human life, that combination of the spiritual and material, the soul makes a final effort to release itself from its limitations and to attain the highest level of self-realization. The material level encompasses unconsciousness in the nonliving, subconsciousness in plants and consciousness in animals. Man encompasses all these levels plus self-consciousness, which makes him aware of finitude and his limitations. The urges from the subconscious also prompt him to work for spiritual development. No other part of creation, divine or material, may exercise this choice. Man can even rise to the level of *Avatara* or Christhood, as Jesus did, to be sent to awaken mankind from its Karmic slumber from time to time. Thus the purpose of reincarnation is ultimate reunion with the Maker. The choice however, rests with the individual himself. Though the aim of the entire creation is gradual progress toward God-consciousness, yet man is the entity who can enjoy the zest of the struggle. His divine seed associates with the evolution of the universe and the Light and Word of God. This dynamic evolution is controlled by the Supreme Person, God.

Human constitution, or the Soul, refers to the individuated divinity, a limited spirituality, a materialized spirit. As such, the soul or entity, which takes human form on our planet (but different forms and dimensions on other levels of the cosmos) is unlike pure material nature. The pure physical nature pervades all creatures other than man, i.e., minerals, plants, animals, birds. This aspect is finally rooted in the Creative Energy or the Creative Mind of God. Its highest indestructible form is *Akasha*, but beings such as minerals, plants, birds, fish, and animals, have no soul in the sense of a unitive principle in their consciousness. In their case death means disintegration into the elements. Their salvation may accrue from a gradual ascent from the most gross physical to the subtlest *Akashic* level, but without any retention of individuality. The divine creation has individuality, but no materiality. Man has both individuality as well as materiality.

Just as God has both internality of immanence in the cosmos and externality of the Cosmic Form, so man has internality of the soul and an externality in body, mind, and intellect. Man is the perfect image of God in this sense. He is a miniature Universe and a miniature Self.

God being Supreme Self, can create and dismiss the entire material, mental, and intellectual aspect of His own Form. But man is a limited self. He is subject to the laws of Karma and reincarnation in his effort to annihilate the lower physical, mental, and intellectual realms of his constitution. But if man sets an ideal before him, if he chooses to follow God's plan, if he directs his actions, emotions, and thoughts toward God, the law of Grace expedites his march in the direction of at-onement with the Maker.

The lower material nature of man consists of eight categories—the atoms of earth, moisture, fire, and gas, plus the mind, the intelligence, and the ego. The higher nature in man consists of the individuated Self. This unitive self, which animals lack, transcends all physical, conscious, subconscious, and unconscious experience. It is continuous even when all the other experiences cease to be, as in the deepest levels of sleep. It is this unitive self of the person which continues to exist after physical annihilation and is reincarnated.

During the reincarnated existences on earth, all the previous experiences, acquired skills, aptitudes, likes, and dislikes accumulated in the previous incarnations, remain in the unconscious aspect of human personality. We shall see later how some of these accumulated tendencies are actualized, while others remain latent, awaiting proper opportunity in future incarnations. Thousands of life readings given by Edgar Cayce are testimony to the theory of reincarnation, and there are hundreds of thousands of such cases collected throughout the world. But the special feature of the Cayce readings is that this testimony has been used for the benefit of the persons whose life readings were given. In India, reincarnation is taken for granted because Hinduism has upheld the doctrine of Karma and rebirth for thousands of years. The theory of the Divine Descent or *Avataravada* also has been elaborated on in the philosophical and religious literature of the Hindus. The doctrine of Karma has been so thoroughly discussed in Hinduism, including its branches of Jainism and Buddhism, that volumes have been written on this subject. With reports of individuals recalling their previous birth and recognizing their previous relatives, homes and even hidden treasures, so commonplace, they do not create any great stir in the East. But this general acceptance is also a handicap. Many interesting cases, which could throw some light on the theory, go undetected. Some of the more recent cases of past memories have been studied and publicized both in India and abroad, frequently by researchers from the West who are beginning to appreciate the ramifications of the phenomena.

The files of Edgar Cayce reveal that there is a practical utility in the discovery of hidden talents and accumulated skills from past births, but a closer study reveals that the readings emphasize God-realization as the true purpose of reincarnation.

Whether Edgar Cayce was giving the life reading of a typist or a musician, a businessman or a would-be intelligence officer, a minister or a teacher, he would invariably come back to the purpose of reincarnation and the theme of at-onement with God. He has stated that each soul is equal in its potentiality for self-realization, even though it may not yet have risen to its perfection due to its wrong choices. The Hindu doctrine of *Karma Mukti*, gradual march toward spiritual liberation, is implied in almost all the life readings given by Cayce. Even though every soul is immortal and God has intended the return of each one of them to their Divine Home, yet the pace of this advance depends upon the use of the will on the part of each soul, independently. The paths of virtuous action, love, and knowledge have been advocated by Hinduism, as well as by Edgar Cayce. Cayce has rendered a great service by reminding man that one should not forget that each individual has to make the best use of his or her talents to fulfill the purpose of God by serving humanity. The gradual spiritual liberation might take thousands of years, but freedom from selfishness, practice of divine love, and selfless service to humanity can speed the redemptive process.

7 ☙
The Doctrine of Karma

In studying the cases of survival claims coming out of the Edgar Cayce readings and other investigation, the question may arise of why the theory of reincarnation should be considered the only explanation of these phenomena. This question might be asked by dogmatic followers of Christianity who have misunderstood the deeper meanings of the words of Jesus Christ, or by the staunch materialists and atheists, who do not believe in the existence of soul at all. Orthodox theologians, who have never compared the reincarnation theory of soul with the fresh creation theory, sometimes join the first, sometimes the second, group. However, the Cayce readings have eliminated any necessary contradiction between the theory of reincarnation and the basic ideas of the Bible, by showing that the teachings of Jesus would be vague and unintelligible without the background of rebirth. With the acceptance of the two theories of reincarnation and Karma, which Jesus is said to have taught in private to his disciples, the Gospels become consistent and logical. But why should we accept these as necessary fact?

We may reply with another question, "Can you prove that the soul is immortal and yet has only a present and future, bereft of a past?" If one believes in the existence of soul, as a noncorporeal immortal entity, he must be confronted with the acceptance of either the fresh creation theory or the reincarnation theory. If it is asserted that God creates a new soul with each birth, is this consistent with a just and loving Father, when some are born blind, some crippled, some retarded? The fresh creation theory cannot explain such miseries, cannot explain evil, cannot explain all the teachings of Jesus, while the reincarnation theory can. Moreover, the latter is logical and scientific and is supported by factual cases throughout the world.

Those persons who have never applied logic to their beliefs about the nature of soul and its fate after the annihilation of the body, hesitate to accept reincarnation. They take on faith the existence of soul and its immortality. Even though their belief does not answer all their questions, they continue to accept it and to oppose the idea of literal rebirth. Contrary to many misconceptions, reincarnation is implied in the Old and New Testaments and does not contradict the communion of departed souls at the nonphysical level, whereas the permanently disembodied future of the soul is incomplete and illogical.

Reincarnation does not mean that a soul must always possess a physical body. It accepts, and even emphasizes, that the soul exists at levels other than material, in other spheres, between incarnations. But the soul cannot attain eternal life until it has paid off its Karmic debts and reaped the good and bad fruits of its past. Paying off the Karmic debts prepares the soul for its spiritual goal of life eternal, the destination of all. No soul was ever created to perish or to be lost. All were meant to be saved. "God did not will that any soul should perish. But man, in his willfulness harkens oft to that which would separate him from his Maker. . . . He has not willed that any soul should perish, but from the beginning has prepared a way of escape! What then is the meaning of the separation? Bringing into being the various phases so that the soul may find in manifested forms the consciousness and awareness of its separation, and (a return to) itself, by that through which it passes in all the various spheres (stages) of awareness" (262–56).

As previously indicated, the sole purpose of reincarnation is the return of the soul to its Maker, but the freedom of will given to the soul, has been the cause of its infatuation with its material manifestation. What then is actually the "way of escape"? The answer to this question is in the law of Karma.

One objection usually brought against the rebirth theory is the evidence of disembodied souls following physical death. Mediums appear to communicate with the dead, indicating that the soul exists in nonphysical form, rather than reentering the material plane, but the possibility of reincarnation does not deny the existence of disembodied souls on levels other than our own. It is not always necessary or desirable for every soul to reenter the earth immediately after physical death, and so there are astral, interplanetary, and intergalactic levels of existence. The object of rebirth is to rid the soul of this cycle of births and deaths by making the best use of its opportunities to love God and man during the terrestrial life. When a person falls short of perfection, he or she might experience other levels of existence and reenter the earth after an interval, realizing that the next sojourn must be utilized as the final escape. Thus, the theory of reincarnation does not preclude several planes of survival, but it does go a step further and states that such intervals are conducive to the awakening of the soul and increase its determination to return to the Maker. Moreover, even during the incarnated state, the soul can be summoned through mediumship while asleep, thus eliminating the final argument against reincarnation.

The fresh creation theory does not withstand analysis as well. Aside from its acceptance of only present and future existence, it fails to explain congenital inequalities. If God is just and good, why must one child be punished with handicaps at birth and another rewarded with extraordinary capabilities? How can we blame God, declaring Him to be partial and unjust, for God is neither unjust nor prejudiced. The immutable laws of nature maintain the harmony of nature and the immutable law of Karma maintains harmony in the spiritual and ethical spheres.

The word Karma has been applied by Edgar Cayce to the effects of actions of a person—those actions which had been performed in previous incarnations. Many other writers on the subject have also used the term in this sense. H. Spencer Lewis has used the term Karma in his book, *The Secret Doctrine of Jesus*, stating that Jesus secretly taught the doctrine to his disciples. He also asserts that the doctrine is alluded to indirectly in many parables given by Jesus to the public during his preaching. Most Western writers are unaware of the fact that a vast literature expounding Karma is available in the Upanishads, the *Bhagavad-Gita*, and most systems of Indian philosophy, dating at least to the sixth century B.C. Let us see how the word *Karma* is used in this literature.

The Sanskrit language has a dynamic grammar, with all nouns derived from verbal roots. The term *Karma* is a noun, derived from the verbal root *Kri*, to do or to activate. Thus, Karma literally means deed or activity. Man engages in activities, by the use of his free will, in three possible ways. These acts are either performed by his physical body, or by speech, or by thought or mind. We see in our daily lives that every act performed by man brings a reaction or effect. According to the law of Karmic ethical causation, all acts, whether physical, verbal or mental, must bear effects. Abuse, either physical or verbal, will be retaliated, usually in kind. Both cause and effect in this case would be called Karma. Even when a person thinks ill of another, he is generating a Karma or a mental action pattern. Frequently the effect of such a mental attitude is discernible. We may intuitively reject the hypocrite who flatters us to our face and slanders us behind our back. But if we resist wishing ill to our ill-wisher, the negative effect of the mental Karma reverts to the originator. Significantly, Jesus Christ has referred to mental Karma in the Sermon on the Mount: "Ye have heard that it was said by them of old time, Thou shalt not commit adultery: But I say unto you, That whosoever looketh on a woman to lust after her hath committed adultery with her already in his heart" (Matt. 5:27–28).

Thus, Karma stands both for the causal action and the effectual action. It stands for physical, mental, and verbal action. But in the context of the doctrine of Karma and its relation to reincarnation, it has still deeper meaning.

In the above quotation, it is evident that Jesus was referring to the immutable law of Karma. This law in the realm of ethics can be compared to the law of the conservation of energy in physics. According to that law, the quantity of physical energy may change form, but the total quantity remains the same. Heat may change into motion and motion into heat, which may in turn change into light or radiation of different frequencies. The physicist relies on mathematical equations to explain the change of energy from one form to the other. This accuracy of calculation confirms our belief that the natural laws of causality support harmony.

Similarly, the law of Karma, which may be called the law of the conservation of ethical energy, is immutable in the ethical and spiritual realms. This law testifies to the harmony in the spiritual world and consistently explains the problems of good and evil and of inequalities in the talents on this earth.

The basic assumption in the law of Karma is that no quantity of the threefold activity or voluntary action, generated by an activity, is ever lost or wasted. Every such voluntary action must bring forth an effect, which is experienced by the agent either in the present life or in any future life. If such an effect or consequence is not presently discernible, it becomes a part of the subconscious mind of the personality of the soul. Such a trait or tendency or future fructification has been called a *Samskara*. The *Samskaras* or Karmic traces, invariably persist in the subconscious mind of every individual soul, life after life. A very large portion of these *Samskaras* remain dormant and inactive in the present life of an individual. They await the proper occasion in a future life to be aroused. But a specified portion of these traits becomes active and must be manifested and experienced by the entity in his present life. Besides these two kinds of Karmic *Samskaras*, every entity (except one who has completed the cycle of rebirth and been saved) adds to the store of his Karmas, new *Samskaras* as a result of new actions. Thus the Karmas are of three categories:

1. Accumulated Karmas or *Sanchit Karmas*
2. Fructifying Karmas or *Prarabda Karmas*
3. Voluntary Karmas or *Kriyamana Karmas*

The accumulated Karmas will be manifested only in the future. The fructifying Karmas must be manifested, experienced and performed, even unconsciously, in the present life, before the soul quits the physical body. Such actions may be modified with effort, prayer, and meditation, but they are unavoidable. They may be termed unavoidable tendencies or even destined tendencies or God's will. Thus in the sense of the experience of their effects, these Karmas are concerned with the present life and not with the future. Normally these Karmas cannot and should not be avoided.

The third category, the *Kriyamana*, or voluntary actions, which are undertaken in the present life, are both present as well as future. Some of these Karmas are immediately rewarded and some of them are added to the accumulation. We should not forget that all these *Samskaras* are generated either by physical, verbal, or mental actions of the entity, in the past or present life. All three types may be good or bad depending upon the actor's intention.

If the *Prarabda*, or fructifying Karmas, of an entity are mostly worthy, the present life will be predominantly happy, prosperous, and spiritually virtuous. Associations, friendships, and even occupation, will be conducive to spiritual development. A voluntary effort to profit by these opportunities may strike at the root of all past Karmas and attain the soul liberation, or eternal life. Thus the entity would finally quit the earth, the goal of all souls. It is in this sense that no soul is meant to perish, as Edgar Cayce stated. The Karmic inheritance or the individual's "burden of the cross" hastens or impedes the salvation.

The essence of our argument is that the doctrine of Karma, instead of being an obstacle to the law of Grace, is its very basis and background. Karma is the means for the development of the soul and Grace is the goal. Karma is the effort, Grace is the prize. Karma is the cross, and Grace is the Resurrection. It is not the power of Karma which has any significance, but the patience of man, which makes him pass through the good and bad Karmas without deviating from the final goal. The shackles of Karma cannot be broken without Grace and Grace is not a free gift. If negative past Karma has caused bondage of the soul and ignorance of man's potential divinity, virtuous Karma with the will to love, can set the soul free. The price is the reversal of Karma from selfish to unselfish, to end the vicious cycle by returning hatred with genuine love, lest the soul be bound by fresh Karmic debt.

The entire Sermon on the Mount is rooted in the philosophy of the reversal of Karma. If we study the Sermon carefully, we see how one idea is linked with another in such a way that the doctrine of Karma is the only explanation of the concept of Christian love. Let us first explain the meaning of love as seen in verses from the Gospel of Matthew: "Ye have heard that it hath been said, Thou shalt love thy neighbour, and hate thine enemy. But I say unto you, Love your enemies, bless them that curse you, do good to them that hate you, and pray for them which despitefully use you and persecute you" (Matt. 5:43–44). Jesus was trying to make the simple masses of his time understand how Grace, which awakens in man the sense of belonging to God, can be invoked by the reversal of Karma. He was emphasizing that love, confined to neighbor or kin, in a reciprocal relationship, is neither good nor bad, but love returned for hatred eliminates a Karmic debt. By this act we become deserving "sons of God." Jesus immediately adds, "That ye may be the children of your Father which is in heaven: for he makes his sun to rise on the evil and on the good, and sendeth rain on the just and on the unjust." This forty-fifth verse of Matthew 5 is in continuity with the previous two verses, and is their conclusion. The sons of God must act like God, beyond Karma, beyond time, space, and causality. The accumulation of past Karmas binds the soul to earth, but it has the freedom of will to return to heaven, the abode of eternal life, free from bondage.

The will of man must be distinguished from the will of God. God's will is that of universal love, without any distinction between friend and foe. Only those who express the will of unselfish love deserve to enter heaven, an interpretation which is supported by the twenty-first verse of the seventh chapter of Matthew which states, "Not everyone that saith unto me Lord, Lord, shall enter unto the kingdom of heaven; but he that doeth the will of my Father, which is in heaven." It is quite evident that Jesus emphasizes the practice of the universal love of the Father. Had he advocated that the Grace of God was free, he would not have preached the practice of God's will by men as the only passport to eternal life.

That Jesus discouraged blind faith is clear in the continuation of the practical attitude in the twenty-second and twenty-third verses of the same chapter of the Gospel of Matthew. The verses declare, "Many will say to me in that day, Lord, Lord, have we not prophesied in thy name? and in thy name have cast out devils? and in thy name done many wonderful works? And then will I profess unto them, I never knew you: depart from me, ye that work iniquity." Here again we see that even though a person may have sufficient faith to cast out demons and work miracles, but does not have universal love for God and man, he does not deserve to enter the kingdom of heaven.

How has the doctrine of Karma been declared as the basis of resurrection? How has Jesus Christ stated that consciously returning hatred with love is superior to blind faith?

The last verses of the fifth chapter of Matthew clarify further. After making it clear that Christian love makes a man a worthy son of God, Jesus goes on to say, "For if ye love them which love you, what reward have ye? do not even the publicans the same?" It is only pure unselfish love, grounded in God, which makes a man free, and leads him toward perfection.

If perfection is the goal of the soul, can it be attained in a single lifetime? Reincarnation must be implied in the Sermon on the Mount. And the law of Karma explains why reconciliation with your brother, to whom you are indebted, is the first step toward God-realization. Verses twenty-three to twenty-six in the fifth chapter of Matthew are testimony to the law of Karma. Jesus remarks,

Therefore if thou bring thy gift to the altar, and there rememberest that thy brother hath ought against thee; leave there thy gift before the altar, and go thy way; first be reconciled to thy brother, and then come and offer thy gift. Agree with thine adversary quickly, whiles thou art in the way with him; lest at any time the adversary deliver thee to the judge, and the judge deliver thee to the officer, and thou be cast into prison. Verily I say unto thee, thou shalt by no means come out thence, till thou hast paid the uttermost farthing.

He warns us that we cannot obtain life eternal, putting an end to the prison of births and deaths unless we have obeyed the law of Karma and paid "the last farthing." Jesus excludes everyone from the kingdom unless the will of God—the immutable Karmic law and divine love—is practiced.

What happens when the will of God is practiced? How does the law of Grace cancel the law of Karma, stopping the wheel of rebirth? What is the meaning of "life eternal," or "the kingdom of heaven"? Is the Grace of God a free gift? These are some of the questions which must be answered. The very fact that Jesus ordered Christians to be "perfect as the Father in heaven," implies reincarnation in his teachings, for how can an individual attain perfection in one life span? The law of Karma and theory of reincarnation are unavoidably linked with man's goal of godlike perfection. "Man is the image of God" because of his potential godliness, but the unfolding of this potential is a gradual process. When the righteous life is accompanied by a strong desire to surrender completely to His will, with the practice of divine love, Grace descends and the aspirant is "saved," while in the physical body. This is called "self-realization" or "the state of being a perfect soul" and is the goal of all spiritual disciplines. All religions claim access to this promised land, but unless a person has experienced the state of spiritual perfection while the soul is in the physical body, he cannot enter the kingdom after death.

What happens to the souls which have made progress toward the goal, but have not reached the climax? What happens to those persons who have come near perfection and have not yet experiénced the descent of Grace in fullness? These souls are reincarnated in families which have a rich atmosphere for continued spiritual development. Some of them await, at higher levels, the opportunity of their final entry into the earth. At these levels they continue to make progress by following the will of God and by imperceptibly guiding the earthly souls in following God's will. But, unless they complete their progress by ridding themselves of all Karmas, they cannot attain life eternal.

At the highest state of spiritual perfection in the physical body, telepathy and clairvoyance occur. The "saved" one is full of love for all existence, full of goodness without selfish motive, undisturbed by threatening situations, free from all hatred, all pride, all greed, and all covetousness. He is free from the desire for false prestige and worldly status; free even of pleasure and pain. In short, a state of complete equilibrium of body, mind, and soul, signals the attainment of this level of consciousness. Meeting such a person, there is an intense attraction and love flows from him to those around him. Such a person has nothing to gain or to lose. He is called *Jivan-Mukta*, the living-liberated, and he is in constant contact with that powerhouse called God, Creative Force, One Spirit. Hé experiences infinite existence, infinite consciousness, and infinite bliss. Thus the Karmas or activities of his body, mind, and speech are ineffective to bind his soul, and he will not return to this earth. He will go to eternal life, the highest mansion in the kingdom of heaven.

Free from all Karmas, accumulated in thousands of previous lives, this liberated soul stays in the physical body as long as he has not exhausted the second category of *Prarabdha Karmas*, or the fructifying actions. In order to understand the issue of fructifying actions, let us go back and review the three categories systematically. We have seen that Karma means both activity or caused Karma, and consequence or effectual Karma. Not all of the effectual Karma, or the consequences of our causal actions, are experienced by us in our present lives. Some are experienced and seen by us, but others are not felt throughout our lifetime. Similarly, we see some effects, some events, happening to us without any present causal action. Some consequences of our conscious efforts seem to have disappeared from the scene. But actually that is not the case. They are on our debit side, to accrue to some future life. The term debit in this context is not meant to be derogatory, for whether we have performed good actions or bad, the effect is a debit, to be paid off in some future. Similarly, we experience events, both good and bad, in our present life without any effort to deserve them. These uncalled for, uninvited and unintended effectual Karmas, are on our credit side of the present life journal. Again, lest we misunderstand, by credit here, we mean effortless fructification. In other words, we must experience some good and bad in our present life which we have not caused voluntarily. For example, all hereditary traits—extraordinary talents or crippling handicaps—all are uncalled for effects due to our past debit and hence, are present credit. The doctrine of Karma and reincarnation explains what the fresh creation theory cannot, inequalities of ability and opportunity, without blaming God, who is just and good.

The threefold divisions of Karma into the past, present, and future, and the relation to credit and debit in the three time dimensions are: (1) *Sanchit Karmas* or accumulated action, (2) *Prarabdha Karmas* or fructifying actions, and the (3) *Kriyamana Karmas* or voluntary actions, which are performed by the individual with the free exercise of will in the present life. The *Sanchit Karmas* are those which were caused by the soul in many past lives and were accounted as debits or liens on the future. But these actions will remain potential, not leading to any effect in the immediate time, awaiting their role in the future. The present is not concerned with them. Normally an individual must be reincarnated to clear these residual Karmas from the record, but when the soul completes its development, Grace descends and all the accumulated Karmas are annihilated. Past and future are eliminated and only the present remains for the soul.

Then why should the soul not immediately attain eternal life? Because the fructifying actions have not been cleared from the account. Whether the soul is that of a terrible sinner or of a saint, whether of an ignorant nonbeliever or of an enlightened theist; whether it is of a confirmed atheist or a devoted lover of God, it must experience all of those Karmas which have started to bear fruit in the present lifetime. Even after Grace has canceled the accumulated actions, these present debts must be paid. No prayers, no meditation, no virtuous life can ever waive them. They are unavoidable and must therefore be accepted with a poised mind, for evasion will only bring about additional reincarnations. But how can we say that a particular Karma belongs to this category? The watermark of these events is that they happen to us in spite of all our efforts to avoid them. This unavoidability, this unexpectedness, and our helplessness in spite of the apparent capability to remedy it are the symptoms of the fructifying actions. These Karmas are the will of God.

With their developed psychic abilities, mature souls may know in advance of these unavoidable events, but they make no attempt to avoid them, for to attempt to avoid such Karmas only binds the soul.

There are many readings given by Edgar Cayce which end abruptly, saying, "We are through for the present," with a subsequent untimely death of the entity. The one cited here shows Cayce, aware of the tragic death to come of a young boy whose reading he gave in 1944, unwilling to shock the parents because he knew the tragedy to be unavoidable. According to the law of Karma, death is virtually fixed and its time, place, and manner depend upon the fructifying Karmas.

The reading by Cayce concerns a boy in London, who was seven years old at the time:

Thus we would confine the direction to the training, the counseling. And then, when the Entity has reached that period of his own choice, or, at thirteen years of age, we would give further directions, if these are sought by the Entity himself.

With all the horrors of destruction, with all the trials in the minds of men in the period through which this Entity and his associates in his early experiences are passing, do keep alive in him the ability to see not only the sublime things of life, but the humor, the wit—yes, the ridiculous also—that may be drawn from the cynic as well as the pessimist, as in cartoons and the like, . . . for in the experience before this, the Entity was a jester in the Court of England, in the name of Hockersmith . . . and set many things in order, when there were those great stresses owing to the selfishness of men.

Also the Entity was among those peoples of Israel who entered the Holy Land, who were married to the Canaanites. Yet the Entity was not among those who led the children of Israel astray. For he forsook Astheroth and served rather the God of Abraham, Isaac and Jacob, as did the one who led the children of Israel through the Red Sea, across the Jordan.

But when the Entity is thirteen years, we would give further directions. Train him especially in English, and at Eton.

We are through with this reading.[1]

Let us see some of the peculiarities in this reading. The first thing to be noted is that Cayce, while describing the horrors of destructions and the trials in the minds of men, which of course were common experiences in World War II, especially in England in 1944, makes a very mysterious observation. He refers to all these horrors "through which this Entity and his associates in his early experiences are passing." According to the record of a newspaper clipping and a letter sent by the boy's mother to Cayce's son, Hugh Lynn, on February 6, 1947, the boy met a tragedy along with a friend. Both of them "ventured into a frozen land; the ice broke and they disappeared together."

In this short reading, Edgar Cayce says that "when the Entity has reached that period of his own choice or at thirteen years of age, we would give further directions, *if* these are sought by the Entity himself." It is noteworthy that Cayce does not mention a next reading, but, rather, uses the word "directions." Moreover, he gives many conditions: "The Entity must reach the age of choice or thirteen years of age and must seek direction himself." Obviously both the Entity and Edgar Cayce must be present at the same plane of exis-

[1]Langley, *Edgar Cayce on Reincarnation*, pp. 111–112.

tence. Accordingly, Edgar Cayce died in 1945, the boy in 1947, perhaps to wait at a lower level of existence for those three years, before reaching the point where he could request of Cayce his "further directions."

In the letter written by the boy's mother to Hugh Lynn Cayce, she went on to say,

My son passed quickly into the other plane of consciousness at about 4:30 P.M., on February 6. I am in the hospital today, expecting my third child. Timmy was looking forward eagerly to "his" arrival and was most anxious that he should be a boy. He also said, a few weeks before he died, "I'd like you to be my Mummy in my next life." I told him he might not be able to arrange that. But he persisted, "I'm going to ask God anyway." I remember answering, "Well, there is no harm in asking." I feel he was well prepared for what we call "death." I had told him in resume the story in *There is a River*, and before that I had simplified for him Stewart Edward White's *The Unobstructed Universe*.

My first thought was that he would come back to us in the body of this tiny baby, especially as I had felt and told my husband that I felt that this baby had no personality as yet, and I wondered what type of soul we would attract this time. . . . I do not, however, now feel that he necessarily will choose to return so soon, even though he "would like me to be his Mummy in his next life.[2]

He could not have returned so soon, even if he had wished so. The choice of the place and the parentage is not always left to the Entity. The very fact that Timmy was born in a family where the atmosphere for spiritual development was congenial, shows that he was directed by the fructifying Karmas. For the same reason, his death was undoubtedly unavoidable. Birth into a particular family, marriage with a particular person, the meeting of a Guru or guide, and death, are always determined by fructifying Karma. As a result of this pattern, the boy was born to a mother who could teach him the meaning of reincarnation. His reading was requested and Edgar Cayce offered to

[2]Ibid., p 112–113.

be his guide when he reached thirteen years. That was fructifying Karma, which matured only after the physical departure of both the Entity and Edgar Cayce.

We have seen that fructifying Karma is that which has its origin in past lives and which becomes effective in the present life of the soul. The accumulated Karmas have nothing to do with the experience of the present life. They are no doubt potentially present, but their realization or fructification must be postponed to future lives.

Another example is taken from Edgar Cayce's readings for the Entity previously incarnated as the celebrity of American history, Alexander Hamilton, who lived from 1757 to 1804. His contribution to the cause of American independence and the framing of the American Constitution is unique. He was a great patriot and a visionary of the future of the new nation. He established the Bank of The United States, as the first secretary of the treasury. He had a vision of the future America as a wealthy industrial nation and this vision has come true in our own time. His work, success and fame indicate that Hamilton must have been an evolved soul. But this Entity, in his most recent entry into the world, as the son of Jewish parents, had to pass through a miserable life, as the following summary will show:

Before the boy was five, his father fell in love with another woman; the parents were divorced, and the mother retained custody of the child. [Broken homes were always somber hazards to Edgar Cayce. He put intense emphasis on the need of every soul to have a secure background during its formative years, and maintained that the preservation of a congenial home was the highest achievement that a soul could aim for in terms of its own progression.]

At the age of twenty-five, the young man was displaying "a very dogmatic attitude about life in general," which a year and a half in the Navy had failed to cut down to size.

The following year found him under psychiatric care and in hospital for shock treatments. His innate tendency to violence had caught up with him. Having met every conflict head-on, he had added to his problems by an impulsive marriage to a divorcee with a child. The repercussions of the broken home revealed themselves here, in that the girl who had broken up his father's marriage and the girl he himself married were of the same ethnic origin, had the same red hair and were both wives of men laboring in the same mechanical field.

When the marriage only served to compound his miseries, he began to suffer belated remorse that he had not kept on friendlier terms with his father during his lifetime. Towards the end of the following year he seemed to feel his only hope of salvaging himself lay in becoming a rabbi, but a further attempt to contact him by the A.R.E. resulted in the return of the letter marked "Address Unknown."[3]

Edgar Cayce had given a life reading when the Entity was only five weeks old, warning the parents that the child would be of erratic temperament when he grew older. In this case we find that the meritorious service rendered by the Entity as Alexander Hamilton had become part of his accumulated or *Sanchit Karmas.* They could not be effective for the Entity, when he was born in this most recent life, because the fructifying Karmas in this birth were the result of remote past actions, dormant in his life as Hamilton. The opportunity offered to him as Hamilton was the result of other fructifying Karmas, but having exhausted their benefit, the Entity was reborn in misery.

The service rendered by Alexander Hamilton must have been his voluntary Karma or *Kriyamana Karma.* This third category literally means those actions which the individual soul performs in the present birth by the exercise of voluntary choice. Volition, or the exercise of will, makes man superior to all other beings. The Entity's birthright, the inherited bodily and mental constitution, the unexpected gains and the uninvited calamities are the result of the fructifying actions, beyond the control of the embodied souls. But man is not mechanically bound by causation, for man's freedom of will makes him *Akala Purusha,* or the Self. Then what sort of freedom does man possess which can release him? We know that some of the maturing Karmas are unavoidable and man must cheerfully face them. God's plan must be accepted with equanimity, which can be done only when we

[3]Ibid., pp 105–106.

exercise our will with reason and intelligence.

The present life of the Entity is like a game of cards. The cards are distributed, each player gets a particular set, and none of them can be changed. But the victory or defeat in the game depends upon the skill and reason as well as the will of the player. The fructifying Karmas provide us with the cards, but the success or the failure of our life depends upon the voluntary actions. Referring to this aspect of man's nature, Cayce remarked, *"But let it be understood here: No action of any planet or the phases of the sun, the moon, or any of the heavenly bodies, surpasses the rule of man's own will power:* the power given by the Creator to man in the beginning, when he became a living soul with the power of choosing for himself."[4]

The opportunity given to the individual at birth can be utilized to choose the path of love and to attain eternal life by acquitting himself of all the fructifying Karmas. The potentiality to shake off all the past Karmas is present in each soul. The Grace of God is the result of the constant effort of the Entity to love God at all times, through loving all human beings, and to attain the knowledge of at-onement with God through meditation. When a balanced life of universal love, selfless service, and the inner knowledge of the unity of the soul with God, leads a man to the state of *Jivan Mukti* or liberation, while the soul is confined to the body, the Entity stands acquitted of all the accumulated Karmas. At the same time, he spontaneously follows virtue and his voluntary actions do not generate any future debit or credit. He is awakened. He attains God-consciousness, becomes god-like, while he continues to live on earth to experience the fructifying Karmas.

The other reason for such a liberated soul to continue to live, even after attaining Grace, is self-purification and to guide less developed souls. The final departure from the earth takes the liberated soul to the Maker. Reincarnation continues to affect all souls, until they

[4]Ibid., pp 130–131.

perfect themselves finally to meet God. Dwelling on this idea, Edgar Cayce remarked, "In the sphere of many of the planets within the same solar system, we find souls again and again and again return, from one to another, until they are prepared to meet the everlasting Creator of our Universe, of which our system is only a very small part."[5] This Creator of our Universe, who as Pure Spirit is the source of the threefold constitution, the divine, the human, and the material, is unaffected by all Karmas. But He, in His infinite mercy and power, does descend to earth as the *Avatara* to remind man of his purpose and to show him the way back to his eternal home, where he can regain his spiritual heritage.

[5]Ibid., p 131.

8 ❧

Avataravada—*The Nature and Purpose of Divine Descent*

God has been given different names in the differing contexts of the major religions of the world. Even in the Bible, God is Love, Light, Word, Bread, Breath, Spirit, Father, Christ, and Holy Ghost. But the basic truth is that God is One. The moment God is individualized as "the God of Abraham," "the God of our Fathers," "your God," "my God," "the Christian God," "the Moslem God," "the Hindu God," we recede from truth. As long as religious denominations continue to emphasize the particular adjectives, neglecting the noun *God*, misunderstandings, dissensions, and disintegration, will prevail in theology. As long as religion is confused with ritual and denominational organization, the adage, "Nearer the church, farther from God," will be true.

Certainly we cannot underestimate the organizational aspect of religion. On the contrary, in my opinion the existence of varieties of religious organizations and activities is a great asset to religion, as an inner experience of life. But at the same time, neglect of the true meaning of religion and overemphasis on institutions and dogmas, in the present age of reason and science provokes a strong antipathetic reaction. Experience and spiritual awakening is the core of religion, with the inner experience providing a base to the external edifice. But when the base is removed, the entire building crumbles. Without spiritual experience, religion is empty and purposeless, while at the same time the present-day social situation encourages cultural rootlessness. The heart of mankind is empty and church attendance as a formality has made religion an object of criticism, frustration, and ridicule. As a result multitudes are turning their backs upon organized worship and finding dissatisfaction, both within the sanctuary and in social activities led by the church. The vacuum of the human heart is bound to seek some substitute for true religion. The sense of purposelessness has made modern society mentally and ethically bankrupt, socially and intellectually bewildered. Mankind is in search of a soul, but this self-discovery, this divine relationship of man with God, this original glory and dignity of the individual, which makes him deserving of the heavenly Grace, cannot be accomplished in prescribed ritual, where more emphasis is laid on structured magnificence than on spiritual awakening and where organization and externalization take precedence over the fact that God is One and omnipresent.

Is God more actualized in one church than another? Or does He reside in every human heart? Is He more satisfied with those who attend impressive services, or with those who experience Him in their simple daily worship? These are some of the questions which we face. We consider modern society to be civilized and advanced because of its progress in science and commerce, yet we exhibit primitive ignorance in religious matters, regarding one denomination or one religion as truer than others, when all believe in one omniscient, omnipotent, and omnipresent God.

These divisive ideas arise because God, the Spirit, the Light, the Word, the Life, and the Love, has rarely been understood, particularly by the orthodox Western world. Overemphasis on the diversities has provoked discord in human society, artificially splitting it into thousands of schools and sects. The statement, "The Lord thy God is One," has been stressed many times in the Cayce readings. Wherever Cayce refers to Christ, he designates him as the Master, and wherever he talks about God, he emphasizes the inner, impersonal, and transcendental aspect of His nature. His message therefore is the message of "unity in diversity." If God is Truth and God is One, as every great religion holds, then why should one community, one denomination, one religion, one race, or one culture monopolize Him? Truth cannot be the property of any race, religion, or nation.

When science has recognized the right of every man to know the truth, why should religious institutions deny the same right? If science, as the search for truth, is transnational, transcultural and transsocial, why should religion not be so? In truth, God is and has always manifested Himself to be universal, cosmic, and objective in the sense of being unqualified by any personal prejudice in every age of crisis. This manifestation of God is also a reminder to the ignorant to surrender their dissension and hatred to unity and love, which are the real characteristics of the Universal God, in whose image man was created. This manifestation of God or the Divine Descent of God on earth has been called *Avataravada* in Hinduism.

The word *Avatara* literally means Divine Descent or Incarnation of God. The word *Vada* means theory or view. The derivation of *Avatara* is from the Sanskrit root *Avatarne*—gliding down or descending. When we say that God has descended or incarnated Himself in human form, we do not mean that God was above the earth or separate from man and has entered into something foreign and alien. If God is omnipresent, as He really is, there is no sense in saying He descends or ascends. Similarly, there is no meaning in saying that the Word became flesh in the person of Jesus. In one sense God is eternally descended and eternally ascended. He is all around. He is present everywhere in all directions and at all times.

Even when capitalized, the pronoun *He* used in connection with God causes great misunderstanding, for as long as God is conceived as a person in the same manner as man, the notion of *Avatara* cannot be grasped. Man has gender, and God, as He, is imaged as male. As one result of this poor understanding of the nature of God, Moslems actually hold that women have no soul. People following blind literal faith in the statements of the Holy Bible have many strange notions about God. They ignore the statements that "God is Spirit," "God is light," "God is life," and imagine God to be a big Person, much like a very large and impressive man, extended throughout space. The manner in which young children are taught to believe literally in the Bible gives Christian youth a poor introduction to the true nature of God. Hugh Lynn Cayce, the son of Edgar Cayce, recounts an amusing anecdote which illustrates this point. Mr. Cayce relates the story of a young boy who had learned at Sunday school that Jesus Christ rose to heaven and is sitting on the right hand of God. In weekday school he read in the primer, "God has painted this beautiful world. He has painted the leaves and the flowers with His own hands." At home, reading this passage to his mother, the boy said, "Mother, God certainly is a wonderful painter. Isn't it wonderful that He did all this with only His left hand?" The embarrassed mother asked, "How did you come to that conclusion?" and the little boy answered, "Don't you know Mama, that God can't use His right hand, because Jesus Christ is always sitting on it?"

The impressions created on children by interpreting the word of God literally are the greatest cause of alienation of the younger generation from religion. Deprivation of spiritual development, which comes from the personal experience of man, does harm to God and to Christianity, which is both a philosophy and a religion. As a teacher of philosophy, I have met hundreds of young American students, who are potentially spiritual and hungry for true knowledge of God. But it is heartbreaking to see that they are disgusted with the church. They feel that the church dogmatically brainwashes them in their childhood. This attitude of young people alienates them from the Bible, which in its true sense advocates the transcendental nature of God as Spirit, life, and love. These frustrated young men and women give up Christianity and do not even know that Christ advocated the universality of God and the love of all men, as the sons of God. This alienation from the Gospel makes them ignorant of the universal truth of the Bible, and the ignorance drives them away from the spirit of Christianity. The result is that they seek other channels, which are sometimes dangerous. Frustration leads to ignorance and ignorance makes them more frustrated. Truth is the only cure for this cycle of bondage. And so, religion must be truth, for if it is not, it will be abandoned. The goal of religion as well as that of science must be Truth—the omniscient, omnipotent, and omnipresent Truth—which religion seeks to uncover and experience.

If we lose sight of this goal, our religion tends to degenerate into narrow fetishism and fanaticism. Instead of being universal, it becomes sectarian. Instead of generating love, it becomes the breeding ground of animosities; instead of offering true knowledge, it spreads ignorance.

Why do we find science making such rapid progress toward truth and gaining the faith of modern man? Why are so many intellectuals fascinated by the success of physics, chemistry, and biology, and acknowledging the superiority of science and technology over religion? Why has the Christian world devoted itself to economic values, while giving lip service to God as Master? The answer to these anomolies from the the spiritually unawakened and chauvinistic scholar, scientist, or philosopher, may be that religion has finally been vanquished by science. Even some Western theologians, in their eagerness to applaud science, are advocating a secular explanation of Christianity.

Certainly there is no need to scorn science, as a material pursuit, and advocate piety as the only truly venerated vocation of man, but I do oppose the fawning attitude of many theologians in the relationship of science and religion. Similarly, I do not approve of the double standard of the scientists, who advocate that the truth of science is superior to the truth of religion. The theologians must cease to be dogmatic and the scientists must give up their claim that the whole truth is discoverable only through analysis, and so-called objective experimentation with molecules, atoms, and electrons.

Both must agree that truth is objective, the monopoly of neither religion nor science, neither of logic, nor of metaphysics. The more genuine and objective the discovery of truth in these different areas of human knowledge, the greater will be the agreement and the unanimity of their conclusions. Science in our own time, has proved that the discovery of truth is progressive and collective. It is the outcome of efforts and experimentation, mutually shared and acknowledged by all scientists, irrespective of their nationality, race, and culture.

Now a similar concerted effort and mutual understanding in religion can lead to exciting discoveries of spiritual truth. However, the religious researcher, like the scientist, must engage himself in the spiritual experiment and report his findings dispassionately, or spiritual truth can be neither discovered nor understood, much less applied in practical life. Authoritarianism, which was a stumbling block in the progress of science for a long time, is now blocking spiritual progress. But a new spirit of mutual understanding among all religions does seem to be awakening all over the world. If we emphasize the biblical statement, repeated again and again by Edgar Cayce, "the Lord thy God is One," then the spirit of truth, referred to by Jesus Christ, will clarify many misunderstandings. Whether the researcher is a Hindu, a Christian, a Muslim, a Jew, or a Buddhist, the spiritual finding will not be repudiated unless and until experience proves it to be other than true.

Let us therefore speak truth in matters of religion and not be afraid of being called heretics. No great scientist, who was creative and original, was ever spared by the reactionaries. Since God is final Truth, let us be patient to hear the experiences of all the lovers of God, for they are also the beloved of God. We will determine not to measure the statements by creed, religion, or race, but by the truth discovered. Just as the structure of the atom is universally accepted and verified by laboratories in all countries, similarly, the experience of God-consciousness shall have to be universally accepted and verified by all without distinction.

We claim that all members of mankind are sons of God, but what actually does the statement mean? We must not commit the error of interpreting it literally, like the little boy, who admired God for painting the beautiful world with only one hand. What is a son? The son is both physically and mentally the continuity of the parents. He has inherited his physical and mental traits from them. In this sense we are all physically and mentally the copy and continuity of God. Not only this, God is our Father, Mother, and the Supreme Ground of the biological, psychical and spiritual constitution of all creatures. In one sense, all beings, living and nonliving, are filled with the presence of God, without whom nothing could ever exist. Not even the Creative Energy, the Cosmic Force, the First Cause, referred to by Edgar Cayce, can exist by itself. God is, in this sense, therefore, infinitely small and infinitely large. He is infinite existence, consciousness, knowledge, power, and love. Thus, His omniscience, omnipotence, and omnipresence are the three strands of His infinite existence, not as a person, limited by body, mind, and individuated Self, but in a super personal manner.

God as Person, *Purusha*, should not be conceived as an individual in monstrous size. This however, does not mean that God cannot appear as a person to His lover. But His appearance as Person or His manifestation as man, e.g., as Jesus Christ or, earlier, as Krishna, should not be considered to be the totality of God. Such an appearance or manifestation is called *Avatara* or Divine Descent. But when God appears physically as a person or as an *Avatara*, His infinite cosmic existence does not cease to be. When the followers of Christ, or of Krishna, or Mohammed, overemphasize the importance of the personal aspect of God and forget that the *Avatara* is simply a manifestation according to the need of the time and place, a fanaticism develops which is actually the very denial of God and the contradiction of all religion. Keeping in view the universal aspect of God, Edgar Cayce has made an attempt to distinguish between Jesus and Christ. In his words, *"CHRIST* is not a man! *Jesus* was the man; Christ the messenger; Christ in all ages, Jesus in one" (991–1, p. 7).

Just as Jesus, the Christ, appeared in a particular age, so was Krishna, the Christ, the manifestation of an earlier age. Christ has been called the *Vishnu* or *Paramesthi* aspect of God. Christ is the only Son of God in the sense that the Christ aspect is the highest and first manifestation of the unmanifest infinite God, which has been called Brahman in ancient Hindu philosophy.

For clarity, let us review the four dimensions of God. The first dimension is called the infinite *Avyaya*, pure spirit, being, the sole ground *(Adhara)* of all existence. As such, God is the ground of the cosmos *(Vishvadhara)*. This aspect of God transcends the spatiotemporal world and remains always untouched by physical changes. The second dimension of God, Brahman, is indestructible absolute, the beyond, *(Paratpara)* aspect of the Supreme Being. At this level God is the efficient cause, the impersonal subject of the creation, One and Absolute. The third dimension of God is the Cosmic Person *(Atmakshara)*. This aspect of God is that of the Creative Energy, the First Cause. Here God is the Creator, still invisible and unmanifested, Supreme Person *(Param Purusha)* standing outside the material world of time, space and causality, possessing the three forces of creation, preservation, and destruction. The personal as well as the impersonal aspects are merged in this dimension. God is yet One, later expressed as nondual Being in whom both the creative energy force of the female and the conscious thought force of the male aspect are merged. The fourth dimension is called the Immanent Spirit manifested in the whole cosmos *(Vishva Rupa)*. The whole spiritual and physical creation is thus the face of God. It is only the fourth aspect which encompasses God as the Master of souls and of the cosmos of time, space, and physical causality.

God as immanent, omniscient, omnipotent, and omnipresent, Ground, Subject and Creator, is the Personal God. His whole Person pervades the cosmos and complements the transcendent aspect, which includes the first three dimensions of God. It is only the fourth, immanent, aspect which enters into personal relationship with individual souls. But this immanent aspect itself has all three transcendent aspects present in it. Using the symbolic image of Father, Son, and Holy Ghost, in referring to the three transcendental aspects of God—the Pure Spirit, the Pure Person and the Pure

Creator—the first is the Father, the second is the Son, and the third is the Holy Ghost. When this God is evidenced, He creates the threefold cosmos of divine, human, and material constitutions, which represent Trinity as immanent. As has been pointed out by Edgar Cayce, man as the image or son of God has the trinity of soul, mind, and body, which is representative of both the transcendent and the immanent God.

Even when God incarnates Himself as a human person, He does not cease to be the Supreme Being. His presence as Father, as the guiding and controlling spirit in the divine constitution, continues to be felt. The presence of God in human insitutions is the Son aspect and His presence in the material world of atoms is the Holy Ghost aspect. Religion adopts the divine path to know the Truth as one God; philosophy adopts the self-realization path to reach the highest manifestation of God in human self; and science adopts the material path of analysis and experimentation to know the same God manifested in atoms, electrons, and motion. But God is beyond all divine, human, and material constitutions. God has always been considered to be beyond human knowledge and understanding, but He is intelligible because the intellectual understanding in man is the flow of the cosmic understanding of the Infinite God.

God as Self is present in divine constitution as Ishwar, Master, Father. God is present in human constitution as Self, or the soul of man. God as Self in material constitution is present as a unitive force as the unmoved motion, faster than the fastest motion and brighter than the brightest light. In the case of the material constitution, the term *Akasha*, which means space, the all-pervasive entity, the ground of all motion, is given to the unitive factor. *Akasha* is at once not motion and infinite motion. Its speed is higher than the highest-moving energy. Although Einstein claimed that light is the fastest-moving energy, scientists undoubtedly will discover some form of energy which is faster. But *Akasha* is the ultimate of speed and stable motion, because in the true sense it is *Purusha*—Self, the generator of all the energy, motion, and change.

In the material constitution the first companion of the *Akasha* is sound, or word, or *Shabda*. Thus, when God is referred to as Light, the reference is to the divine constitution; when He is referred to as Word or Sound, the reference is to the material constitution. Similarly, when God is called Love, the reference is to human constitution, since love is the result and effect of the soul, or the great Self. The great Self represents the galactic center of the divine constitution in man. Thus, the Light aspect of God, the first companion of God in the divine constitution, is the Vishnu or Christ aspect. It is this which incarnates itself when it descends in human form with all divine qualities. This is *Avatara*, the perfect manifestation of God in human form.

Avatara, or the Divine Descent of God, has been taking place on earth for ages to remind the individual souls that they are all originally divine and their goal is God. The soul, whether in divine or human constitution, manifests itself in individual form to be the companion of God. But it becomes involved in the material constitution and forgets its original divine home. Edgar Cayce expresses a similar idea in one of his readings: "In the beginnings, or in the activities in which the soul manifested individuality, it was for the purpose of becoming as a companion of Creative Force or God; or becoming the whole body of God itself, with the ability—even as thy Pattern, as thy Savior, or as thy Guide and Guard—to know thyself to BE thyself, yet one with Him." (1650–1).

This reading of Edgar Cayce beautifully depicts the purpose of the Divine Descent. Without the previous discussion of the nature of God, this reading might not be understood by the reader in its true philosophic and metaphysical sense. We have stated that all men are the sons of God. The words "Creative Force" and "God" can now be understood by the reader as One Immanent God, the unity in trinity, the Father, Son, and Holy Ghost, expressed in the three constitutions. We have stated that just as man is the son of God in human constitution, Christ or Vishnu, the ruling Self of the galactic center, who incarnates his Self in human form as *Avatara*, is the Son of God in divine constitution. When Cayce says that the individual soul, i.e., man, has ability to be itself one with God, "like the Savior, the Guide and the Guard," he is simply stating what we have said in connection with the relationship of man with the Immanent God. The purpose of the Guide or the Savior in incarnating Himself in human form is to awaken slumbering humanity to Divine Consciousness.

The words "to know thyself, to be thyself, yet one with Him," in the above reading have a deep metaphysical significance. Note that Edgar Cayce is referring here to the nature of God as the Supreme Person, or *Purusha*. Man is his own individual Self and in that Self he is rooted in the *Purusha*. But at the same time, man is one with God, because the same deep-rooted *Purusha* in him is the continuity of the infinite Supreme Being, who is transcendent as the ground of the cosmos, and who is immanent as the Source of all creation in the threefold constitution.

Thus man is potentially divine and materially limited. Our discussion of the threefold creation and of the nature of the human soul indicates that man is both infinite and finite. His finitude makes him bound to Karma and reincarnation. His infinitude urges him to attain his divine form of oneness with God. Edgar Cayce has expressed a similar view of man in the following words: "Hence we find the mental body is both finite and infinite, a part of self and yet a part of a universal consciousness—or the mind of the Maker" (1650–1).

The *Avataras* in every age tried to awaken the Self-consciousness, or the divine potentiality of man. The message of the Self-awakening in every age was brought to mankind in keeping with the need of that age. It would be difficult and even impossible for us to give the account of all the *Avataras* and all the messages received throughout the ages. But we shall refer to at least four such incarnations, to explain the four categories of the Divine Descent. These four are Rama, the ethical messenger; Krishna, the messenger of ethics and love; Buddha, the messenger of nonviolence and peace, and Christ,

the messenger of peace and love. These four *Avataras* present to us
a continuity in the fulfillment of God's purpose or will on earth, but
our main discussion will be confined to the two great *Avataras* of
Krishna and Jesus Christ.

9 ❧

The Theory of Divine Descent—
A Message For All Ages

Avatara is the Divine Descent of God, the manifestation of God in human form. More precisely, the *Avatara* is the representation of the Son or preservative aspect of God. God's threefold character of Creator (Father), Preserver or Sustainer (Son), and Destroyer or Purifier (Holy Ghost) are accepted both by Hinduism and Christianity. Preserving and sustaining implies compassion for the preserved and the function of the *Avatara* is compassion or love.

Because the galactic center and its offshoot, the sun, represent the preservatory or Christ aspect of God as immanent in the spatiotemporal world, the *Avataras* associate themselves with light as the center of the galaxies and of the cosmos. Lord Krishna, historically about two thousand years prior to Jesus, says, "Among the suns, I am galactic center" (Vishnu—the Christ aspect). Jesus similarly states, "As long as I am in this world, I am the light of the world." Uninformed persons may take the word "light" metaphorically, in the sense of something that removes darkness; however, the reference is to a concept of greater significance.

Throughout history, the *Avatara* is called the Lord, which is the descriptive title of an *Avatara*. In a broad sense, a prophet is also an *Avatara*, as is every man. But an *Avatara* of the Christ aspect of God is called the Lord, *Bhagavana*. The term *Bhagavana* is rooted in the explanation of the macrocosmic aspect of the threefold manifestation of Immanent God in the cosmos. We have stated that there are five dimensions in one branch of the cosmos—cosmic center, galactic center, sun, moon, and earth. Actually they represent motion in these respective regions. An *Avatara* must be the controller of all these regional motions and must possess qualities which indicate such power. But at the same time, he must also be unattached to all cosmic and material creation. So an ideal *Avatara* must possess the following six *Bhagas*, or qualities:

1. *Vairagya* or nonattachment (corresponding to the transcendental aspect of God)
2. *Jnana* or true knowledge (corresponding to cosmic center, the Father aspect of Immanent God)
3. *Aishvarya*, or mastery (corresponding to galactic center)
4. *Dharma*, virtue or ethical duty (corresponding to the solar aspect)
5. *Yasha*, fame (corresponding to the lunar aspect)
6. *Shri*, kingship (corresponding to the earth aspect of God)

The complete *Avataras* do possess all the six qualities mentioned, but the *Avataras* have different aims at different ages. Hence, they may differ in the manifestation of the qualities as well as in the endowment of some powers, because of the differing situations under which they appear. There are at least three categories of *Avataras*. The first category manifests preservation only; the second, the awakening or preceptorship only; and the third category manifests both the preservation and the preceptorship. In this chapter we shall concentrate on four *Avataras* only. Chronologically, the first is Rama, who represents the preservatory manifestation of God and emphasizes ethics and virtue (though love is implied throughout). The second example is Krishna, who combines the preservatory and the preceptor aspects, representing love and ethics combined. The third example is that of the Buddha, who represents the preceptor aspect only (though love is implied in it). The fourth is of Jesus Christ, who again combines the preservatory and the preceptor aspects and conveys virtue as well as love.

RAMA AVATARA

Rama Avatara is chronologically the oldest in our selection. In the absence of any concrete evidence, the date of this Divine Descent may be put between 5000 B.C. and 4000 B.C. These dates are suggested on the basis of the internal evidence of the Vedas, Upanishads, and the other sources of Sanskrit literature. The Western scholars have always tried to bring the dates of prehistoric Indian history forward. But these theories are inconsistent with the facts, recent excavations, and the internal evidence of oriental Indian literature.

The word *Ram* literally and etymologically means "that which pervades the whole world." It indicates the omnipresence of God. Ram has been described from four points of view by one of the greatest poets of India, Tulsidasa, as follows:

> *Ek Rama Dashrath Ka Pyarya;*
> *Ek Rama Jag Jis Ka Pasara;*
> *Ek Rama hai Palanhara;*
> *Ek Rama Duniya Se Nayara.*

> or
> One Rama is the son of man;
> One Rama is the Creator immanent;
> One Rama is the preserver of norm;
> One Rama is the transcendent.

This verse affirms the point that an *Avatara* is the human manifestation of God. God, the transcendent, is Pure Spirit, unaffected by the spatiotemporal changes—the Father aspect. God, as the preserver, is the Christ, or son, and God, the immanent cause, is the Holy Ghost. The Christ aspect is called the Vishnu in Hinduism, and

Rama is recognized as the manifestation of Vishnu. In every age, God has manifested Himself through the *Avataras*, differing His revelation because of the infinite nature of God. To say that God has revealed Himself only once at one particular place or in one particular age is to degrade the supremacy and infinitude of God. God's manifestation as Rama was not the totality of the *Avataravada*. Every Hindu, educated or uneducated, recognizes and understands this truth. Rama, as the manifestation of the Supreme Being *(Param Brahman)* and as the personification of Vishnu, is worshiped by all Hindus in general and the devotees of Rama in particular. We must be clear here that the worship of Rama, which consists in singing, communion, and the discourses on the sacred *Ramayana*, the complete story of Rama, does not mean worshiping Rama, the human being. Rama is seen as Supreme Being, omnipresent, omnipotent, and omniscient. The human form, which is the manifestation of the Supreme Person, is also historical, as the manifestation of Christ, as Jesus, is historical. God, being omnipotent, can and does show Himself in the person of Rama to the true devotees, who enter into a personal relationship of love and self-surrender, as God-intoxicated or Rama-intoxicated. They see the presence of God in all creatures. The great poet, Tulsidasa, says:

> *Siya Ram Maye Sab Jag Jani*
> *Karun Pranama Jodi Jug Pani.*

> Because the whole cosmos is replete with Rama [God]
>   and his wife Sita [Power aspect of God]
> I salute every one in the world.

This poet who wrote the great work of the *Ramayana* in Hindi verse in the sixteenth century, was himself God-intoxicated. The original *Ramayana* is an old work, written in Sanskrit, and the Tulsi *Ramayana*, the work of Tulsidasa, is to Hindus today, like the King James version of the Holy Bible for many Christians. This work is not merely biographical or literary, but is the epitome of the Hindu philosophy, religion, ethic and culture. This work has also been translated into English verse by a non-Indian Christian missionary and is available in India from The Hindustan Times Press, New Delhi.

The power aspect of God is an integral part of Himself, and significantly, in the case of three of the four examples of the *Avataras* being presented here, we have evidence of that power of God, being manifested in the form of a woman, accompanying the *Avataras*. In the case of Rama, it became his wife, in the case of Krishna, his senior playmate (who had a pure spiritual devotion for Krishna, devoid of carnal desire) and in the case of Jesus this power aspect was manifested in the person of the Virgin Mary. Edgar Cayce mentions in one of the readings that the Virgin Mary was a part of the soul of the Master, "In the beginning Mary was the twin-soul of the Master in the entrance into the earth!" (5749–8).

Another important fact is that Rama, as well as Krishna, presents the ideal for every man. The purpose of reading the *Ramayana* is to absorb the virtues of Rama and to try to attain the same level of ethical development. Similarly, with Krishna, the Buddha and Jesus. There is a continuity of the ideal and the message conveyed to humanity through all the four.

The detailed story of the *Ramayana* is unnecessary here. The literature on the writing, both as an epic and as a religious work, is plentiful. Rama was an ideal son, brother, husband, friend, king, and father. His life affirms that if a person is dutiful in all the spheres of life, in spite of suffering, and remains truthful in the performance of all duties, he can attain spiritual perfection and ultimately, life eternal.

Born a prince, Rama's subjects loved him. His father planned to anoint him Crown Prince, since he was the oldest son, and a date was fixed for the great ceremony. However, Rama's stepmother, Kaikeyi, at the instigation of a jealous maidservant, intervened. Kaikeyi had once saved the life of her husband, King Dasharatha (Rama's father) on a battlefield. While the king was fighting, the axle of his chariot had broken loose. In order to save her husband, the brave queen held the wheel fast with her hand, resulting in the loss of one of her fingers. The king, learning of her bravery, and wanting to reward his beloved wife, asked her to demand three favors. But Kaikeyi requested that the granting of the wishes be reserved for some proper occasion. Now, when the coronation of the Crown Prince Rama was announced, her maidservant persuaded the mistress to invoke the favors, demanding that Rama's coronation be postponed; that Bharata, blood son of Kaikeyi, be anointed Crown Prince; and Rama be exiled for fourteen years.

King Dasharatha, who loved Rama deeply, fell unconscious and soon afterward died, from the shock of the demands. But Rama dutifully told his stepmother that he would immediately prepare for his exile. Unfortunately, Bharata, her son, who had always loved Rama, was not present, and so the prince and his devoted wife, Sita, completed their plans to leave the palace and the town. Another younger stepbrother, Lakshmana, who loved his older brother, also decided to accompany him to exile. When all three had left, with the subjects mourning, Bharata arrived home. He was shocked to find his beloved father dead and his older brothers gone. In his devotion, he searched the forests and finally found the exiled group. Earnestly and humbly he begged Rama to return to the capital to take charge of the kingdom. But to fulfill the promise given by his father to Queen Kaikeyi, Rama declined the offer. Rama in turn, pressed Bharata to assume the reins of the government for fourteen years, and to this he agreed, with one stipulation. Rama must leave his sandals behind, so that they might be put on the throne as evidence that Bharata would act only as the custodian of his older brother's kingdom.

During the last year of the exile, a tyrant, Ravana, the devilish king of Ceylon, carried Sita away, in the absence of Rama and Lakshmana, from their forest home. Knowing that Rama was the incarnation of God, the demonic king expected his own tyranny to be compensated by his death at Rama's hands. Thus, he kept Sita a chaste captive, and, in spite of Rama's demands to release her, Ravana purposely refused. Ultimately Rama, with aid of an ally king, was compelled to wage war on Ravana. The king, before dying on the battlefield, confessed his tyrannous deeds and expressed his respect for Rama, as the *Avatara*.

The fourteen years being over, the exiled party returned to the capital, which celebrated the return of the ideal king by illuminating the town, still commemorated in the festival of Divali. The rule of Rama was marked with justice for all and adherence to truth. Justice was administered without distinction or prejudice and the king often would visit the town in disguise to ensure that no one was oppressed. The ideal moral administration of justice in India is still called *Rama Rajya*, the rule of Rama, which makes the people equal and fearless, honest, loving, and forgiving.

What is the significance of *Rama Avatara*? It emphasizes that happiness here and liberation hereafter can be attained by adhering to one's duty, with full faith in God. That was the message of Rama, who was himself the embodiment of virtue. Why should one be moral? Not because morality is imposed by authority. Not because of external pressures; not because it is a social contract. The sole purpose of virtue and duty is the integrated development of human personality. When a code of conduct is imposed as a social tradition, without any purpose of self development, the individual is bound to revolt against it. The conflict between the individual and society cannot be resolved, either by reducing the former to a mere cog in the social machinery, as in a totalitarian society, or by regarding the individual as a rootless, self-centered entity, unconcerned with the plight of others, as is implied in an extremely individualistic society. The only solution can come from the recognition of the station and duties of each person, whose goal is the integrated development of his own self.

The message of Rama aims at social harmony and goes a step

further by assuring that virtue is at the same time the necessary condition for spiritual evolution, ultimately leading to life eternal. Rama is therefore called the *"Maryada Purushottam,"* the propounder of the attainment of human excellence through ethics or duty. Thus, adherence to virtue is not an outer legislation, but an inner urge; not a formal confirmation, but an experimental verification of the truth, which ultimately brings about the union of the individual soul with God.

KRISHNA AVATARA

Krishna Avatara, the Divine Descent in the person of Lord Krishna, is significant because the message delivered by him is universal, encyclopedic, and applicable to all ages. In this revelation, the manifestation of the Divine Power is present in its fullest form. This *Avatara* combines, in himself, mastery over natural laws and over human nature, as well as universal and spiritual love and preceptorship of the highest order. If Rama is regarded as *Maryada Purushottam,* or the embodiment of ethical excellence in man, Krishna is *Leela Purushottam,* the revealer of spiritual excellence, unaffected by material nature, in spite of being physically, ethically, and socially involved in human affairs. He shows that, like a lotus flower, which grows and blossoms in marshy water, but remains untouched by it, a man may lead an active life in society and fulfill all worldly obligations, yet remain free from attachment, through constant contemplation and love of God. This attitude of transcendence gives a proper place to the relative ethics of right and wrong in human needs and human thinking. There is no doubt that the path of transcendence, which is the stage beyond good and evil, is through ethics, through virtue, good, and righteousness. But these ethical steps are less than the goal to which they lead. The goal is transcendence, infinite love, and infinite bliss. When a climber reaches the top of the highest range of mountains, he does not ignore the existence of the smaller peaks through which he passed during his ascent. But having reached the highest peak, their significance fades. If the climber imagined them to be insignificant without reaching the top, he would never transcend them. On the other hand, if the climber were to mistake the lower peaks for the highest ones, he could never rise above the lower level, because he took the means to be the end.

Morally, as long as man remains on the ethical level, without turning his gaze upward, he is bound by the cycle of lives and deaths. Reincarnation is both an asset and a liability. The appearance of the soul on earth in human form is an opportunity for it to attain life eternal, or *Moksha*, and so, even the most highly developed souls are reincarnated. But the loss of the memory of previous spiritual development may make any soul indulge in material play, taking the worldly life to be the end of human existence. The love of the material world, of eating, drinking, and sex, intoxication of power, wealth, and social status, the pride of physical strength, personal beauty, and intellectual achievements, are not only the temptations, but the golden, invisible fetters, which bind the individual soul to the cycle of reincarnation. While these experiences are unaccompanied by the knowledge of soul and God; while man remains egoistic, and devoid of love, he continues to return to physical, mental, and intellectual suffering. And so, society is plagued with maimed, blind, dumb, mentally retarded and criminally inclined persons. The individual must utilize the opportunity of human birth by leading a balanced life—the life of enjoyment without indulgence, dynamic action without attachment, and deep love without emotional depletion. All this is possible, according to the life and philosophy of Lord Krishna. His philosophy integrates the practice of spiritual knowledge, ethical virtue, and divine love.

Krishna Avatara, called *Purneshwara*, or the Perfect Master's *Avatara*, was endowed with all the divine powers, which he could utilize from infancy to protect his devotees. As he grew up, he gained complete knowledge, both through education under the perfect teacher and through the practice of yoga. The activities of Lord Krishna throughout life were extraordinary and imbued with a deep spiritual attitude of unattached love. These activities of his are called *Leela* or play, and he is *Leela Purushottam*, the divine manifestation in the form of human excellence in play. The active participation of Lord Krishna in all the stages of his life, was in fact, deeply suffused with spiritual love for all. He was conscious of being detached from the effects of his activities and maintained an innocence and purity of soul. The perfect personality, with a deeper knowledge of ultimate truth, could see that all activities of the world of time, space, and causality, are merely the play of the Supreme Spirit. The purpose of his Divine Descent was to demonstrate through his life how an ideal person could perform his role successfully in the Universal Play of God.

In the absence of definite dates, the time of Lord Krishna's appearance on earth can be estimated between 2000 and 1500 B.C. All the events of his life are detailed in *Shrimad Bhagvat Purana*, and in the great epic, *Mahabharata*. The greatest teaching of the *Bhagavad-Gita*, which runs into seven hundred verses in old Sanskrit, is a part of this epic.

Krishna was born in the city of Mathura, which is about eighty miles from New Delhi, on the bank of the river, Jamuna. Just as Jesus is reported to have been born in a manger, Krishna was born in a jail in similar circumstances. Krishna's mother, Devaki, was the sister of King Kansa, tyrant of Mathura, who had usurped the kingdom of his own father and imprisoned him. Kansa had been warned by the astrologers that one of the eight sons of his sister, Devaki, would kill him to relieve the people of his oppression. So Kansa took great care to kill the first seven sons of his sister. Each time she conceived, Kansa would confine her and her husband, Vasudeva, to jail and would release them only after the child was killed.

The birth of Krishna, eighth child of Devaki, took place at midnight, and the guards, in spite of the strict instructions to be vigilant, went to sleep. The locks of the prison automatically opened and the huge iron doors stood ajar.

At the time that Krishna was born, Nanda, a close friend of Vasudeva, was blessed with a daughter, across the river Jamuna, in a village called Gokul. Vasudeva placed his infant son in a basket and walked out of the prison. He crossed the turbulent Jamuna, which subsided immediately when its water touched the feet of the infant. Vasudeva reached the humble house of his friend safely and exchanged his son for the newborn daughter of Nanda, who was brought to the jail before dawn. In the morning King Kansa was startled to find a daughter born to his sister. His sister and brother-in-law begged him to spare the life of the girl, but the cruel king would not listen and killed the baby mercilessly, as he had killed his seven nephews. This time, however, a voice announced, "You tyrant, your conqueror has already been born, you cannot overcome him!" Next morning Kansa ordered that all the children born within those few days be killed, but Krishna was not discovered. Later Kansa learned that the child Krishna, who was being brought up by Nanda in Gokul, was his eighth nephew. He made attempts to have the child killed, but each time he failed to accomplish the evil deed.

Krishna's childhood was spent among the cowherds, much as Jesus lived among the shepherds. He studied the Vedas, the Upanishads, the philosophic literature, and was recognized as the "king of the yogins." The yoga propounded by him has been beautifully depicted in the *Bhagavad-Gita,* the Song Divine. Its message is eternal, universal, philosophical, and pragmatic. It reconciles the domains of science, philosophy, and religion, and offers a beautiful synthesis of the spiritual and secular aspects of human life. This philosophy is an answer to the perpetual problem of the conflict of duties in the modern conditions of life in East and West.

The opening scene of the drama that leads to the formulation of the philosophy of the *Bhagavad-Gita,* is one which presents and poses an ethical problem. The scene itself is enacted on the field of battle, named the Dharma Kshethra, the field of duties. The author of the *Mahabharata*, the sage, Vyasa, who declared that "there is nothing superior to man in the cosmos," begins the first chapter by putting these words in the mouth of the great King Dhritarashtra:

Dharmakshetre kurukshetre samaveta yuyutsavah;
Mamakah Pandavascaiva kimakurvata Sanjaya!

O Sanjay! What did my sons and the sons of Pandu do,
having gathered in the field of battle, the field of
righteousness [duty] with the desire of war?

The battlefield is referred to as the field of righteousness or duty here for two reasons. The first is semihistorical and the second is philosophical. Folk history tells that the five Pandavas, first cousins of the sons of Dhritarashtra, had been denied their right to property, having lost everything in a questionable game of dice to the Kauravas, the sons of the king. The five brothers had left the kingdom for thirteen years on the explicit understanding that their territory would be returned to them at the end of their exile. The dispute arose when the Kauravas permanently appropriated the entire kingdom of the Pandavas. The Kauravas, particularly Duryodhana, the oldest son of the king, would not accept any prior claim and would not grant even five acres of land to the Pandavas for their subsistence. Thus, Duryodhana claimed to be right, holding that the Pandavas had lost their kingdom at the game of dice; and Yudhisthira, eldest Pandava, claimed to be right, because in spite of being tricked, he had fulfilled the terms of exile. When all the negotiations failed, both parties decided to settle the issue at Kurukshetra, the battlefield; hence the name field of *Dharma*, or duty.

The philosophic significance of the field of duty is obvious. The classical systems of Indian philosophy, and the Vedas and Upanishads, unequivocally accepted *Dharma* or socioindividual duties as necessary and unavoidable for ethicospiritual development. Each individual must attend to his duties according to his social status, psychological inclination, and the profession adopted by him. *Varna*, or caste, of an individual was not determined by birth, but by these three. In the *Bhagavad-Gita* this fact is clarified by the great yogin, Krishna. The classification of caste was entirely based on profession and the bent of mind of a person, during the epic period. But once that person had adopted a particular calling, it was necessary for him to adhere to the duty enjoined, even at the cost of his life.

Even further, the opportunity of laying down one's life, while performing one's duty, was a golden chance for attaining liberation. This opportunity of dying on the battlefield, particularly for the Kshatriyas, or warrior class, is regarded as entering the open gates of heaven. Thus, when King Dhritarashtra refers to the battlefield as the field of *Dharma*, he has in mind the courting of death, as the highest duty. Deviation from duty is regarded as the most heinous crime, both by Arjuna, the pupil, and his preceptor, Krishna, the propounder of the philosophy of the *Gita*.

We may sum up the message of Lord Krishna, by stating that there is no antagonism between spiritual and secular life. Self-control means harmonization of desires and the subordination of body to mind, mind to intellect, and intellect to God. Man is capable of attaining God-consciousness and maintaining an attitude of nonattachment, while he is actively and officially engaged in worldly affairs. The message of Krishna was both philosophical and spiritual, because it was directed to the people, who could understand and practice the ideals. At the same time, it was universal, because the path of love does not need any philosophical background. The most striking message delivered by him in the *Bhagavad-Gita* is the reference to *Avataravada*, "When the extreme indulgence in unrighteousness and vice overshadows righteousness and virtue, at that time I incarnate Myself . . . in every age. A person who knows the secret of *My* Divine Birth and Activity in this context, is freed from reincarnation, after he lays aside his physical coil, because he come to *Me*."[1]

[1] *Bhagavad-Gita*, IV, vss. 7–9.

Thus, the *Avatara*, or Divine Descent, has a specific purpose and message according to the time and place. The message so conveyed is both particular and universal. It is particular, because of the spatio-temporal situation in which the *Avatara* appears. It is universal, because the message is a continuity of the revelation of God, conveyed to human beings through all the *Avataras*. The Buddha and Jesus Christ were in keeping with this principle of spatiotemporal necessity and the universal continuity of the message and revelation to mankind.

The Buddha

The *Buddha*, literally the Enlightened One, was the *Avatara* which succeeded Lord Krishna. The message of Krishna of the spiritual equality of mankind had been forgotten and inequality and hatred had reached a climax in India. The need of the hour was a straightforward approach to *Moksha*, or liberation, without any intricacies of metaphysics, rituals, and institutions. Hence, the Buddha based his philosophy on the ethics of nonviolence and righteousness. His awakening was the result of his longing to find a remedy for suffering humanity, and he called *Moksha*, *Nirvana*, which literally means freedom from all sufferings.

The *Buddha* was born Siddhartha, the first son of King Shudho-dhan. He was brought up with great caution and love, because the astrologers predicted that he would renounce the world to travel and preach. Being the first son, the royal parents were keen that Siddhartha should become the ideal king, and the idea of renouncing secular life was abhorrent to them. So every care was taken to provide the growing prince with all the comforts and luxuries. From the beginning of his life, the boy was compassionate and loved all nature. At maturity, he was married to the most beautiful princess of his time, Yashodhara. The couple loved each other deeply, and when their son, Rahula, was born the parents of Siddhartha were confident that the prince would never be estranged from the world. But none of these events could check Siddhartha's destiny.

One day the prince decided to visit the town and the king arranged for the public appearance with great pomp and show. The streets were cleaned and the subjects were ordered to greet the prince with rejoicing and songs. All precautions had been taken to keep ugliness and misery away from Siddhartha's sight. But fate delivered, at the first stop, suffering in the form of a sick man lying on the roadside. Never having seen illness, Siddhartha was astonished to learn that the man was in agony from a terrible disease. "Is there such suffering and sickness in the world?" he asked.

At the second crossing, the prince's attention was drawn to a wrinkled, halting old man with a stick in his hand. Moved with compassion, the prince asked, "What has happened to this person?" The attendant replied, "Oh noble prince, he has grown old. He is ninety years of age. His body has grown weak and he has lost the power to see, hear, and walk. Everyone who grows old suffers from these defects." Siddartha mused, "Old age—another suffering in the world."

At the next crossing, the body of a young man of a wealthy family was being taken to the cremation ground. Siddartha heard the cries of the wife and children and the groans of the relatives. He asked again, "Why are the people crying? What thing is being carried by the men on their shoulders?" The prince was told that the bier contained the corpse of a young man who had died; that the family was crying because he would never come back and that death is a necessary end of every human being.

This was the greatest shock of all to the young prince, who had never heard of death before. He returned to his palace and considered seriously the sights he had seen with a growing longing to find a remedy for them. In the dead of night, Siddartha made his decision to set out in search of truth. He bade a silent good-bye to his beautiful sleeping wife and son, and quickly walked out of the royal palace, never to return again as a prince.

Under the guidance of several teachers, he practiced the ascetic life for twelve years, only to find that his body was reduced to a skeleton, but he had not found his answers. Siddartha gave up fasting and went to quietly meditating. One day, while in contemplation under a large banyan tree (afterwards to be called the *Bodhi*, or "cause of awakening"), he was enlightened with the four noble truths or *Arya Satyas* and thus became the *Buddha*—the Enlightened One. The first noble truth revealed is that there is suffering in the whole world; secondly, there is the cause of suffering; thirdly, there is the cessation of suffering. The fourth truth is the way to put an end to this cycle and to attain *Nirvana*, complete freedom from all suffering.

According to the Buddha, attachment is the sole cause of suffering in the world and the remedy lies in leading a life of righteousness and meditation, without any selfish motives. He laid great stress on nonviolence, which, in positive form, means love and compassion. In one of his dialogues with his pupils following initiation, the Buddha said to his disciples, "While you are preaching the noble truth, some persons may abuse you and even humiliate you." The disciple immediately replied, "Sir, I would still love them, be compassionate to them and thank them, because they have not, at least, injured me physically."

The Buddha went on, "It could be that some of your audience become violent. If some of them throw stones at you and injure you, what would be your response?" The pupil calmly answered, "I will endure the injuries and still bless them, because they have not killed me."

The Buddha added, "Suppose some persons are very fanatic and they kill you. What would you think of them?" The pupil replied with confidence, "I would still love them and bless them, because the physical coil is the only hindrance between myself and *Nirvana*. I must be grateful to the persons who help me to reach the final goal."

This persistence of the positive attitude was the core of Buddha's teachings. He was so overwhelmed by the sufferings of the people, caused by their own ignorance, that he was prepared to sacrifice everything to bring them enlightenment. His last words were, "Oh

God! If the sufferings of the people of the world can be transferred to me, I am prepared to take them and relieve all the souls of their burden."

These words are noteworthy, because the next *Avatara*, Jesus Christ, not only wished that the sufferings of the whole of humanity be transferred to him, but also demonstrated that he could sacrifice his body and earthly life, so that love and peace might be upheld as the symbols of Divinity, as the necessary and unavoidable factors for the survival of mankind. What was the need of the Divine Descent of Jesus Christ, so soon after that of the Buddha? We should remember the words of Lord Krishna, who stated that in every age, the Divine Descent takes place, when people forget or misinterpret the universal message.

Buddhism spread rapidly in Asia. Thus the *Dharma* of piety, as it is called, was welcomed by the whole of Asia, especially in the third century B.C. The spiritual King Ashoka sent the Buddhist missionaries from India to all parts of Asia, including China, Japan, and Malaya. As a result, most of the Asian countries became Buddhist. The ethics of Buddhism was attractive and appealing. It was based on nonviolence and truth. But with the passing of time, Buddhism tended to become skeptical and nihilistic. Different schools and sects of Buddhism arose, the basic notion of nonviolence was neglected, and the Buddhist countries outside India colored the philosophy according to their local prejudices. In India, Buddhism died out as Hindu philosopher Shankaracharya, defeated Buddhists in debates over God and man's relation to God. The whole of India was reconverted to Hinduism without bloodshed. Although Buddhism had advocated the love of mankind, of *Ahimsa*, the metaphysics of the faith was very weak. There was great need for the positive message of Divine Love, workable and practicable for all humanity in daily life.

JESUS CHRIST

The last great *Avatara*, or Divine Descent, was in the person of Jesus Christ. The birth of Jesus was preceded by prophecy similar to that of Krishna, and similar legends surround his early life. Jesus did have a thorough spiritual training, but whether this training was given to him in his native land or in India, Persia, and Egypt, as the Edgar Cayce readings have indicated, is not especially significant here. At least eleven years of his very early life have not been accounted for in the Gospels. Rosicrucian sources, *The Aquarian Bible*, and the Cayce readings agree that Jesus did go to India and had training with the sages. *The Aquarian Bible* and the Rosicrucian-published literature state that young Jesus was sent directly from Carmel to Jaggannath in India, under the escort of the wise men.

Certainly, during the first century B.C., Jaggannath was an important center of philosophy, culture, and religion, with its temple dedicated to Lord Krishna. This city, now called Puri, is still one of the four headquarters of the four Shankaracharyas or chief pontiffs of the Hindu religion. The word *Jaggannath* means the master of the cosmos. There is no doubt that during the first century B.C., Hinduism had degenerated to its lowest ebb, but there was no dearth of spiritually advanced teachers in India. That Jesus Christ should have gone straight from Mount Carmel to Jaggannath, seems quite possible, even though there is no direct evidence to establish it as an authenticated historical event. If Jesus did have his training in India, as a preparation for his ministry of universal love, this fact should be a threat neither to Christian nor to non-Christian, for the Divine Descent always has a universal purpose, though it is motivated by specific conditions in different ages.

This universality of the message, conveyed through the *Avataras* of the past, is significant today, because science and technology have made humanity a closely knit community. In the words of Jesus Christ, "And other sheep I have, which are not of this fold; them also

I must bring, and they shall hear my voice; and there shall be one fold, *and* one shepherd" (John 10:16).

If Jesus Christ was the Son of God (as surely he was and is), could these remarks refer to the Jews alone? If the message of Christian love is not directed to the whole human race, then Christianity can never be accepted as a universal religion. Jesus Christ could not have been unaware of the highly developed religions of Asia, even if it is denied that he went to India for training, and the Cayce readings indicate throughout that Jesus Christ cannot be confined to any particular time or place. The Christ aspect of Jesus, the universal aspect both of his personality and of his missions, is the continuity of the divine manifestation, the purpose of which is to invoke the potential Christ in every human being, so that he may ultimately unite with his Maker. God-consciousness or Christ-consciousness alone will prove that Christ, the shepherd, is within every individual, just as "the kingdom of heaven is within" every person. The chief difficulty for all the separated religions is that they are unaware that the shepherd who has to lead them to one flock is potentially present in every member of the fold. There is no harm in having many folds, but the trouble arises when each fold begins to labor under the delusion that it is the entire flock, while many members are deaf to the voice of the shepherd. If all members of all folds would listen to the voice of the shepherd within their own hearts, they would realize the unity running through the diversity of all religions. In addition, the voice within every individual can enkindle divine love in human hearts and end their conflicts and sufferings.

How can this voice be heard within? How can one awaken from the illusion of belonging to one flock, when actually one does not even truly belong to the fold? Jesus Christ answered this question in the Sermon on the Mount and through the life of love and truth which he lived. The answer is not so simple and it needs more than one lifetime to act upon it; but through meditation, the effort to live and love positively, and complete self-surrender to God, summed up in the command to "love the Lord thy God, with all thy heart, and with all thy soul, and with all thy mind," the inner self can awaken even in one life. When Christ says that he is the way to God, he means that his life as Jesus, revealing the awakening of the universal Christ in everyone, is the way.

Consider the words of Jesus, "Verily, verily I say unto you, I am the door of the sheep" (John 10:7). If by the person of Jesus Christ, we mean the historical Jesus, the statement signifies that the life of love for God and man, which Jesus preached and practiced, is the doorway to God. This was in fact the temporal, historical purpose of Jesus Christ's incarnation or *Avatara*. The universal, unselfish love which overlooks all faults and weaknesses in its object, is the result of the awakening, which raises the ordinary man to a Christlike state. Hence the statement also implies the enkindling of the Christ Spirit or the potentiality of the divinity or Christ-consciousness in man.

What is meant by saying that Jesus Christ is the "door of the sheep," in the exemplary sense? We know that Jesus was extraordinary in history, for praying to God for the forgiveness of his murderers. He did not hate anyone, whether they were socially or morally defiled, or even violently opposed to his views. He returned hatred with love, contempt with respect and practiced his ideals by refusing to resist evil, by "turning the other cheek." We recall that the adoption of a positive love toward one who hates us without provocation also implies that we put an end to the cycle of Karma. Apart from this, the emphasis on love, accord, and reconciliation has a great historical significance, even from a secular view. It is true that universal love cannot be generated in all the hearts of the world overnight. However, even a highly advanced soul experiences gradually higher levels of the divine love. That love and the adoption of the positive attitude in all of life is imperative now.

Today mankind has reached a stage where any major war involving atomic weapons would put an end to life as we know it. A positive attitude of love on the part of all statesmen who are in control of the nuclear power of the world is essential for the safety of the human race. In other words, Jesus Christ as the way, even in the secular value of adopting positive patterns of understanding and good will, appears to be the only basis of peaceful coexistence, with the only alternative codestruction.

Summing up the universal message, conveyed through the Divine Descent of the four major *Avataras*, we may conclude that it was the revelation of the will of God in four different phases, each one being supplementary and also universal and integrative. The sole purpose of the message is to awaken man, to lead him back to the Final Truth, the Maker, the First Cause. This Truth is one, because "the Lord our God is One." Rama, Krishna, Buddha, and Jesus—all four are emanations from the same Truth and represent the Christ aspect of God. It is in this sense that Edgar Cayce has remarked in one of the readings, "Hast thou not found that the *essence*, the truth, the *real* truth is *One?* Mercy and justice; peace and harmony"; *"CHRIST* is not a man! *Jesus* was the man: Christ the messenger; Christ in all ages, Jesus in one, Joshua in another, Melchizedek in another; *these* . . . that led Judaism!" (991–1).

The four *Avataras* summarized here revealed the fact that truth is one and that man's goal is the same truth, the same one God. Analysis of the different contexts in which these *Avataras* appeared leads us to the conclusion that truth is to be sought through the practice of the virtues of duty, balance, enlightenment, and love. Rama set the example of adherence to ethical and social duty. Krishna exemplified the balance of the spiritual and secular virtues, which combine duty with love and self-surrender to God; the Buddha, the Enlightened One, aimed at wisdom through the practice of righteousness. Jesus Christ emphasized the practice of love, which embraced the human and divine aspects of man. Thus the four *Avataras* collectively emphasized the integrated development of human personality and the attainment of liberation, or life eternal, or at-onement with God.

We are reminded that man is not only a finite being. He is infinite as well. As the image of God, he is potentially divine and inherently pure. He is the combination of the macrocosmic and microcosmic forces. What he needs is self-discovery and self-realization. Reincarnation, or his appearance on earth in human form, is not the end but the means. He must therefore adopt the best possible technique to accomplish the goal of God-realization, Krishna-realization or Christ-consciousness. We will see in the following chapter the significance of meditation as the technique which leads man to God.

10 &

Man, Meditation, and God

In the message of Rama, Krishna, Buddha, and Jesus Christ; in the teachings of the Vedas, Upanishads, and Bible, we hear a recurrent theme—that man is the highest manifestation of God. Man has inherited divinity from that source and although he has wandered, he retains his potential divinity and inherent infinitude; his only goal is to regain his original glory and to rekindle his Christhood. In the words of Edgar Cayce, ". . . man has been made just a little lower than the angels; with all the abilities to become *one with Him!* not the whole, nor yet lost in the individuality of the whole, but becoming more and more personal in ALL of its consciousnesses of the application of the individuality of Creative Forces, thus more and more at-onement with Him—yet conscious of being himself." (2172–2, p. 2).

What defines the species man? Why is he considered superior to all other living beings? Is it his superior body? His superior mind? His superior intellect? Lions and elephants are stronger; the cobra and turtle are far longer lived. Even in physical beauty, many animals surpass man and the oceanographers tell us that there are creatures of great delicacy thousands of feet beneath the sea.

Then perhaps man is man because of his mind or intelligence? But even mind, with its feelings of pleasure and pain, fear and anger, is equally shared by animals. The cunning of the jackal and panther indicates their intelligence. The porpoise has as complex a brain as

142

man. But man has something more valuable than even intelligence. It is that something more, that basis and ground of unity, that self or soul, which makes man a self-conscious, spiritual being, who, in spite of his physical handicaps, mental frustrations and intellectual confusions, is capable of self-realization.

Man, as complete man, is an integrated whole of body, mind, intellect, and soul or self. The fourfold nature of man propounded here is based on the analogy between man and the cosmos presented earlier. Since Edgar Cayce has included intellect with mind, later we shall combine the two for the sake of convenience. Cayce, however, offered the same philosophy with the same purpose, of defining man in terms of his soul, irrespective of the activity of his body, mind, and intellect. He says, ". . . know that no urge, no sign, no emotion—whether of a latent mental nature or of a material or emotional nature finding expression in the body—surpasses that birthright, will—the factor which makes the human soul, the human individual, DIFFERENT from all other creatures in the earth, from all manifestations of God's activity!" (2172–1, p. 2). The words "latent mental nature" refer to what we have been calling intellect; the expression "emotional nature" means mind. It is quite clear in the reading that man's distinctive characteristic is soul.

The "birthright," freedom of will, is both an advantage and a disadvantage. Man is superior even to the *Devatas* (natural forces or angels) which have no freedom of will, when he harnesses his will to that of God and practices divine love. But equally, when this will is misused, the purpose of his incarnation is lost. He produces destruction and devastation, because he has forgotten the core of human nature, wrongly identifying with body, mind, intellect, and ego, which are only appendages of the soul.

The soul force is unitive; its first characteristic is selfless love—love for God, the divine constitution; love for man, the human constitution; love even for natural creation in the material constitution. Man only strays from the course of love when he deludes himself that he, not God, is the master. The sole purpose of religion must be to make man aware of his soul, his indestructible, unitive self, to lead him to spiritualize the secular life and to divinize his flesh and animal nature.

The neglect of the inner religious experience and the emphasis on formalized worship have alienated today's youth. A typical college student has expressed his honest reaction to the gulf that exists today in the profession and practice of religion. A student of Christopher Newport College, Newport News, Virginia, Corky Tierney, in his article, "In the End," writes:

In the end man destroyed both the heaven and the earth.

And the earth was without form; and devoid of all life, and darkness was on the face of the deep. And the spirit of God was stilled upon the face of destruction.

On the first day of the beginning of the end Man said, "Let there be light," and the Atom was upon us . . . and multitudes were incinerated. . . . And Man said, "Let this light divide firmament from firmament" . . . and hundreds of thousands cried for what was Hiroshima and Nagasaki, and the evening and the morning were the first day.

On the second day Man created insecticides and herbicides and . . . he destroyed the grass, the herb-yielding seed, and the trees bearing fruit and . . . those six and eight-legged creatures that crawl upon and in the earth and Man . . . said, "It is good."

On the third day Man created structures of steel and glass and paved the earth with . . . all manner of foul things and choked the life from the earth and allowed it to run off into the waters. And Man saw what he had done and called it good.

On the fourth day . . . Man went out into those few areas left unspoiled by Him and He destroyed all animals and winged fowl and dumped raw sewage . . . in the waters and . . . eradicated "the great whales and every living creature that moveth and every winged fowl." . . .

On the fifth day Man destroyed all incentive for productive labor by creating Welfare and Negative Incomes . . . and he took his hates . . . to the heavens and orbited all manner of garbage . . . around the earth . . . and He polluted what . . . had been clean and untouched by Human greed and malice. . . .

On the sixth day Man destroyed Himself. First He destroyed all those not sharing the One belief and then He destroyed all those not of His own kind through enslavement and hate and then He destroyed Himself with tobacco and alcohol and by ingesting drugs . . . which are foreign to his body . . . and He died. And His dried and bleached bones had dominion over the stagnant waters and the smog choked the air and it was good. And the evening and the morning were the seventh day.[1]

This parody shows the sincere concern of the young writer for the future of mankind and the right use of will power. Neither true religion nor church is the cause of such reactions. There is a genuine urge for truth and God in every man, and the strong desire to fight against suffering disease, old age, and even death is indicative of the indomitable and eternal element of the spirit, which is the special characteristic of man.

The word "man" is the equivalent of the Sanskrit word *Manava*, which is derived from the root *Mana* or *Manu*, which literally means the center of unity. When this center of centers is recognized, the relativities of loss and gain are transcended. An equipoise, which gives unique strength to human personality to withstand all the stresses of life, becomes a constant habit with a man who has realized the Self in his own self. That Self is the real existent personality. But if it is neglected, kept from spiritual food and exercise, its potentialities are never actualized.

Repression of any of the aspects of man's being will lead to the unequal development of human nature, resulting in the ills of the present age. Why is the human race still beset with terrible physical and mental diseases, in our age of science and technology? Why is there poverty in the midst of plenty, hunger in the midst of gluttony, and growing shortages of basic materials in the midst of colossal waste? Is man honest with his own self? Or has he never cared to know what the real Self is? An overwhelming majority of people do not even rise beyond the physical level of existence, not to mention to the height of their being, the soul. Some do develop their minds,

[1]"In the End," *The Captain's Log*, No. 1, Oct. 14, 1969, p. 2.

and a few among these achieve high intellectual development, but how many ever care to develop the spiritual aspect? How much time, money, and effort do we expend in discovering the spiritual Self in us?

A baby is normally born weighing seven to eight pounds but continuous feeding and exercise result in a fully developed adult. The healthy mind—feelings, instincts, and desires—should develop similarly, but in affluent countries mental illness is a serious problem. The cases of neuroses, psychoses, divorce, homicide, and suicide, which are increasing in number, are indicative of the imbalance of mental life. Psychologists warn us that if we do not feed the mind properly, satisfying the urges and desires naturally, mental abnormality will be the result.

We are, in addition, urged to provide training and food for our intellectual faculties. Levels of intellectual accomplishment differ according to opportunities and natural energies, but years of academic education, encompassing thousands of hours, might enable an especially gifted person to become a renowned scholar. It is certainly agreed that no achievement is possible without a continuous intellectual effort and training.

But even though a person builds a sound body, a healthy mind, and a quick intellect, if he has not given food to the soul, he is an infant in spirit. That is why the world's successful people, a Marilyn Monroe with a beautiful body, or a Hemingway with a brilliant mind, may commit suicide. Without nurturing the controlling spirit, the core of human personality which produces harmony of body, mind, and intellect, real happiness and peace here, and blessedness hereafter, can never be realized.

"The kingdom of God" experienced within man results in material, mental, and intellectual, as well as spiritual awakening, which leads the individual from unreal to real, from annihilation to immortality. But how many persons discover divinity in themselves? How much time, effort and training is expended to activate this unlimited energy, knowledge, and joy? If you ask an average church-going man what effort he has made and what training he has undergone, he might report a lifetime of regular church attendance. But that church, instead of telling the devotees that "man is the image of God" and that "the kingdom of God lies within" human personality, places its emphasis on fear and sin, which are associated not with the soul, but with mind and body. The bewildered seeker may then reject the church and look for an answer somewhere other than the House of God. Without guidance and direction, he may resort to occult practices, psychedelic drugs, and unrestricted indulgence in sex. The hollowness of modern man is the result of neglect of the soul and its powers of healing, love, wisdom, and harmony.

Meditation is both the training and the food for the soul, developing its potentialities, proving its existence, and, above all, providing the means of Christ-consciousness. In other words, meditation has a twofold purpose of self-realization and God-realization. It produces a harmonious development in secular life and also recovers the glory of the soul and at-onement with God—the Supreme Person and the Supreme Goal—the real home, to which man originally belonged. Without the attainment of this living ideal, no one can enter the kingdom of heaven, as Jesus Christ has preached. This is the way—the only way. This is the state of *Jivan Mukti*, liberation while alive, salvation on earth.

Thus, meditation is a technique and a methodology, not an interference in the metaphysical beliefs and ethical commands of any religion. Theologians in the West who have stressed a ritualistic, dogmatic Christianity have grossly neglected the significance and role of meditation. The result is that religion becomes dogma and secular ethics, halfheartedly acknowledged as the way to God. Though the word meditation is not unknown to Western religion, its real import is not recognized, even by the most highly educated ecclesiasts.

Edgar Cayce's great importance lay in his effective emphasis to the Western world on the significance of meditation as the way to Christ-consciousness or self-realization. The Association for Research and Enlightenment has compiled material from the readings for the guidance of those who want to practice the way. The minimum time to be devoted, according to this code, is fifteen minutes, which is a good beginning and is helpful for the average Westerner who is rushed for time, but is not really enough for higher spiritual development. The advantage of this beginning is that the aspirant can later increase his time and effort and can ultimately reach the highest state, called *Samadhi* or yoga. In Eastern cultures, the fifteen minutes' meditation is called *Dhyana* or focusing of the attention, which in its highest and most intense state is transformed into *Samadhi*. Edgar Cayce's description of meditation encompasses both practices.

The term *Samadhi* is a Sanskrit word, as is yoga. *Samadhi* is derived from the root *sam*, equalization or balancing, and *adhi*, controlling. *Samadhi* therefore means controlling the various aspects of human personality to produce equilibrium. The word *yoga* is derived from the term *yuj*, to unite or harness. The English word *yoke* is derived from the same root and has the same meaning as yoga. (Incidently, the pronunciation of the word is "yog," with the "a" silent.) Yoga means uniting with the Cosmic Consciousness or the union of the individual soul with God.

All the systems of Indian philosophy, including those of Buddhism and Jainism, in spite of the differences in their theology and metaphysics, unanimously accept yoga as the sole method of spiritual awakening or self-realization. *Samadhi* or yoga is intensely empirical. It is not discursive or analytic, but intuitive and integrative. This technique or methodology alone can give us the knowledge of the Self, for how can we analyze this unanalyzable soul? How can we subject the unitive and continuous Self to the divisive and discursive methods of the physical sciences or mathematical calculation? Only by the intuitive and integrative method of meditation can we know the knower, and become conscious of the experiencer of consciousness.

If the word yoga is defined as the tuning of the self to Cosmic Mind or Creative Energy, it can have a very wide connotation. This tuning could be conscious or unconscious, voluntary or involuntary. It could be systematic and methodical or haphazard and naive. The term *yoga* cannot correctly be used for the involuntary, haphazard, and naive tuning of the self to the spiritual realm. While I do not deny the possibility of casual glimpses of spiritual powers experienced by psychics and drug users, and I am not minimizing the importance of dream analysis and symbology, as a preparation for meditation of higher type, I must categorically state that the avenues other than meditation should never be considered yoga. The danger is that the psychic experiences through means other than meditation usually lead the experiencer to indulge in these for their own sake and thereby slow down the pace of inner growth. However, the very existence of these experiences is both a challenge to the skeptic and an assurance of the discovery of the spiritual self to the aspirant.[2] These experiences, including those of the recall of previous incarnations through hypnosis, all occur frequently and cannot and should not be brushed aside by science. The scientific explanation of these phenomena, and the philosophic enquiry into their causes and conditions, would undoubtedly throw light on the nature of the soul. Meditation or yoga ultimately leads not only to a systematic and controlled experience of all of them, but also gives a direct knowledge of their source and brings about at-onement of the individual self with the Cosmic Consciousness.

As an analogy, let us accept that a variety of melodies, beautiful scenes, and interesting people are available this instant in the very room occupied by the reader. But the reader is oblivious to all if there is no radio or television set in the room. But we cannot deny the potential presence of the sounds and scenes, for it can be actualized if we have the proper receiving set and if we switch that set on. Similarly, every human soul is a highly sensitive and reliable receiving set. The only flaw is that it has not been switched on or tuned to the Cosmic Current. When it is attuned, sounds and sights, messages and events are experienced and the potentiality of the soul to rise

[2]These phenomena include automatic writing, telepathy, precognition, clairvoyance, clairaudience, out-of-body travel, postcognition, etc.

above time and space is actualized. This is what happens when systematic meditation is practiced. In this manner the characteristics of the soul, like those of the atoms and electrons, are demonstrable and verifiable, because the soul, switched to its Source, overcomes artificial limitations in its knowledge and apprehension and even in the scope of its love and affection, thereby perceiving the true meaning of the teachings of Christ.

In this way meditation helps the secular as well as the spiritual life. It ultimately spiritualizes the secular and generates an inner and outer harmony. The efficacy of the discipline becomes discernible in a physical, mental, and spiritual metamorphosis which should encourage the experimenter to adopt the regular practice of yoga. Though every normal individual has a longing to experience the truth of the soul, in this age of skepticism and reflective thinking, urging may be necessary. It must be emphasized that meditation as a technique is not mere theory but is objective—every human being has equal possibilities of applying it successfully and in arriving at equal results. Whatever rules or prerequisites are suggested in this brief account are the result of experimentation on the part of those who have succeeded in its application.

The term *yoga* is vast in its connotation, and there are many approaches to its attainment. Out of a great variety, there are three main types: (1) the path of knowledge or *Jnana Yoga*, (2) the path of action or *Karma Yoga*, and (3) the path of love or *Bhakti Yoga*. A combination of all three paths is called *Sammattva Yoga*, or the integrative path which Edgar Cayce presented. This yoga has been highly spoken of and advocated throughout the *Bhagavad-Gita*. *Hatha Yoga* is another kind of yoga, which consists in a very strict physical training. It needs great caution and guidance, because of the possible harm should the inflow of creative energy be too sudden. But a few steps of *Hatha Yoga* (literally meaning hard yoga), particularly the movement of the neck, some postures of the body and the breathing exercises can very easily be incorporated into the integrative method. All the paths of yoga can be called *Samadhi Yoga*, the meditational path, because their ultimate goal is the attainment of the highest stage of meditation.

In the beginning, it is necessary to devote a fixed time and later to increase the extent of meditation for real achievement and enlightenment. Ultimately the aspirant reaches the stage when a fixed time is no longer necessary because he is constantly attuned—while walking, talking, eating, drinking, sleeping; while reading, writing, and praying. This stage, called *Jivan Mukti*, or being free while in the physical body, is the indication of the soul's salvation. Without this indicator, one can be sure that after death the soul shall have to be reincarnated. The very fact that we have been incarnated and are present at the earth plane, proves that we have not yet been saved in this sense—"saved in this sense" because no soul has ever been created to be destroyed. In one of the readings, Edgar Cayce stated, "God does not will that any soul should perish. . . . *He* has not willed that any soul should perish, but from the beginning has prepared a way of escape!" (262–56, pp. 3, 4).

Note that the way of escape was prepared from the very beginning. Lord Krishna said that the way of escape, yoga, was known in past ages, but it was forgotten in the passage of time. He also declared that he had appeared many times and had explained the path of escape many times. He was not referring to his limited human personality as Krishna, but the universal Christ or Vishnu in him.

The positive definition of meditation or yoga is attunement, or harnessing the self to God. The negative definition points out that the goal of meditation is to rise above all spatiotemporal limitations, including those of intellect and ego. Meditation therefore must disentangle the pure soul from all the relativities, physical, and mental. As such it has been called *Chittavritti Nirodha*, the stopping or blocking of all the manifestations of the individual consciousness. It is interesting that Edgar Cayce has given both the positive and the negative definitions, which correspond with the two given in the Hindu philosophy. Referring to meditation as the attunement, one reading says, "It is not musing, not daydreaming; but as ye find your bodies made up of the physical, mental, and spiritual, it is the attuning of the mental body and the physical body to its spiritual source" (281–41, p. 1).

This definition of meditation is what is called *Laya Yoga*, the path of attunement. The Cayce readings mirror the fact of the various avenues of self-realization. Yoga, in the broader sense, is nothing but the awakening of the infinite Self of man. The following reading illustrates Cayce's agreement:

"Then, there must be a conscious contact with that which is a part of thy body-physical, thy body-mental, to thy soul-body or thy superconsciousness. The names indicate that ye have given it metes and bounds, while the soul is boundless—and is represented by many means or measures or manners in the expressions in the mind of each of you" (281–41, p. 2).

The fact that the goal is higher even than the superconsciousness will become apparent as we proceed in this chapter as well as in the concluding chapter, "Beyond Karma and Reincarnation."

Hence, yoga or *Samadhi* is the technique used to rid one's self of all relativities of the consciousness, as defined by the great sage Patanjali, who laid down a complete science of yoga. Agreeing with this transcendental definition, Edgar Cayce states, "*Meditation* is *emptying* self of all that hinders the creative forces from rising along the natural channels of the physical man to be disseminated through those centers and sources that create the activities of the physical, the mental, the spiritual man. . . ." (281–13, p. 4).

In order to reach the knowledge of the relationship of the soul to God, it is necessary to follow a spiritual discipline, which is the prerequisite for the technique of meditation.

Enthusiasm or sincere curiosity is the prerequisite for any undertaking in the field of human experience, and particularly in meditation. The more intense the interest, the quicker the success, for psychological studies indicate clearly that interest and attention are interrelated, and the first stage of *Samadhi* is attention, although conversely, attention sometimes becomes the source of interest.

Since man does not know many of his own potentialities, especially the extension of his psychic powers, when, he succeeds by attention and effort, in developing some of his talents, his interest naturally increases.

The Cayce readings have been of great help to many individuals who were unaware of their latent talents. Some of those persons, told of their unknown abilities in a particular field, denied them and declined to explore the suggested interests, only to distinguish themselves later in that very profession or occupation. The greatest latent powers in man are the spiritual powers which lie deep under the layers of his subconscious and unconscious mind. Constant effort is necessary to remove the debris of ages of reincarnations that has dimmed the light of the spirit. Grace no doubt is the instrument of final purification, but is Grace so cheap that it should be squandered on the lazy and careless? God's love is no doubt unlimited. If we go one step, He advances a thousand. Once we have made our connection with Him, His Grace pours on us from all sides. But in order to arrive at that moment, we must sincerely adopt the proper rule of life.

The preparation for meditation may be summed up under three headings: (1) Physical; (2) Mental; (3) Spiritual.

Physical Preparation

Since the body is the temple of God and the house of the soul, it needs to be healthy and clean internally as well as externally. For internal health and cleanliness, the aspirant requires a balanced diet, which should be neither too rich, nor too poor. However, it is best to avoid heavy meat such as pork, ham, beef, and even lamb, because of the basic elements contained in them.

There are three basic elements or forces in food: (1) *Sato Guna*, or lightness, corresponds to inward motion or preserving force; (2) *Rajo Guna*, or activeness, corresponds to expending of energy or outward motion; and, (3) *Tamo Guna*, or heaviness, laziness, corresponds to stability. Light foods are best for preparation for meditation. All heavy meats produce toxins and are in the third category. Intoxicants result in laziness and are definitely to be avoided. Milk, fruits, vegetables, and eggs (particularly as a meat substitute for Westerners) are the most desirable foods. Fish, lentils, beans, tea, and coffee all have the *Rajo Guna* element and are not harmful when taken moderately.

The person who is in the habit of eating heavy meats, as most Westerners are, is not banned from the practice of meditation, and will actually gain from it, but experiments show that when heavy foods are curtailed, progress is noticeably speeded. In addition, food prepared at home is preferable to commercially prepared or restaurant food. This may sound strange to the "eat-out-often" American, but it is important because the mood and the mental constitution of the cook influences the effect of the food on our minds. Thus, a housewife should affectionately and cheerfully cook and serve the family meals. Light exercise in the open air and regular walking with deep breathing, in conjunction with light diet, is a good preparation for the proper internal conditions.

Four rules for external aids to physical health are: (1) Normal sleep (five to eight hours); (2) Avoiding overindulgence in sex; (3) Resorting to special postures; and, (4) Breathing exercise.

There are no hard and fast rules for sleep, but a person who sleeps more than is necessary will be lazy and slow in spiritual progress. Breathing exercise remarkably compensates for sleep. Let us therefore review the recommended system.

Inhale slowly—very slowly—counting one, two, three, four . . . in your mind. When the lung is full, start to exhale, counting again. If, while inhaling, you have counted ten or fifteen or twenty, then while exhaling very slowly, count to twenty, thirty, or forty, for a ratio of one to two. Start with a count of ten and gradually increase the count to twenty within ten days. The count of twenty should continue for a year or two and thirty should be the limit. Note that if the inhalation is from the left nostril, exhalation should be from the right, and vice versa, alternating each time of meditation. Besides being useful for preparation, this exercise is a good prescription for many ailments of the respiratory and cardiovascular systems.

The instruction concerning sexual activity is not based on any associations of guilt, for the normal enjoyment of sex in married life is helpful for physical and mental health. Rather, the caution is against overindulgence, which reduces physical energy.

The third discipline is in bodily posture. It is helpful to sit on the floor with the body erect and legs folded in front. This posture aligns all the seven centers, or *Chakras*, of spiritual energy in the body and gives a strong base to the first of the centers. However, if this is difficult, one should sit in a straight chair with body erect. Normally one can continue to sit in this posture for fifteen or twenty minutes with no strain. With regular practice one can remain comfortably for an indefinite time. The length of meditation should gradually be increased from fifteen minutes to one hour or more, which will occur spontaneously with increased experience.

Mental Preparation

Mental discipline is also ethical discipline. In the West, ethics has often been associated with external influence, with a resulting rebellion against authority. But man's free will does not give license for unrestrained impulses. Human freedom is superior to that of animals precisely because man is capable of imposing some limits on himself. Such a self-imposed discipline is beneficial to our mental health, to our intellectual progress and to our spiritual awakening. The five principles of restraint to be observed are: (1) Adherence to truth; (2) Adherence to nonviolence physically, mentally, and verbally; (3) Adherence to honesty and self-help; (4) Avoidance of sexual indulgences; and (5) Restraint from greed or avarice. The positive principles of forebearance, contentment, and universal friendliness are three additional rules for mental preparation. These rules of mental and ethical discipline should never be accepted as external commands, but as spontaneous modes of behavior. The closer these rules are followed, the quicker will be the progress, and with more progress ethical behavior becomes more spontaneous. Thus the interaction of cause and effect form an upward spiral leading to mastery over the self. The practice of the combination of wisdom, love, and meditation so metamorphizes the physical and mental personality that virtue and happiness become an integral part of the blissful life.

Spiritual Preparation

Self-study, God-consciousness, and prayer form the triad of spiritual preparation. Self-study, which here means the study of the literature of all the great saints and saviors, is the most important prerequisite in the spiritual discipline. A study of the lives of the prophets and mystics of Christianity, Hinduism, and Islam will build confidence in the mind of the novice, who will discover unity in diversity and the Oneness as the goal of all religions. But all this is only a preparation.

The second step in the spiritual preparation is the love of God and self-surrender to God in daily behavior. With a constant recollection of each man as the image of God, we automatically overlook the faults of others. Only then can we return hatred with love, purify the soul, and prepare to enter into communion with God. This self-purification, eliminating ill will, allows us to meet God in our daily human contacts, recognizing Him in each person we encounter.

Prayer has a unique place in spiritual preparation. It is the supplication, the earnest invocation and the dialogue of the soul with the Maker, who is eagerly awaiting our companionship.

Prayer is an attempt to tap the imperceptible current of Grace. The more earnest, the more selfless, the more submissive is the prayer, the more effective it is. But the prayer of preparation should not be a supplication for anything other than Grace and Love and Compassion for the awakening of the soul.

Both silent and spoken or sung prayers are appropriate aids, but simplicity of language is quite as effective as literary metaphor, since an omniscient God knows our desires even without verbal expression. Even a sincere resolve to pray for Grace may be sufficient, but prayer itself is instrumental in awakening the physical, emotional, and intellectual urge to see God face to face.

Edgar Cayce suggested that chanting *Om* or *Aum* or *Haree Om*, while preparing for meditation sets up positive vibrations. In these sounds Edgar Cayce pronounced the words of the highest Mantra of the sages of ancient India, the final and most supreme secret of attuning the soul to God. For *Aum* means God, the Spirit-Father, and *Haree* means Christ or Vishnu. *Om* or *Aum* is the basic creative sound resonating in the entire divine constitution, just as the sound *Aham*—I AM—is the underlying resonance in human constitution or man. Thus the vibrations set up by the chanting of *Om* attune the soul to God. In the instructions issued in some ARE pamphlets, it has been suggested by the editors that the *Om* chant may be replaced by music. Unfortunately, this suggestion is based on the ignorance of the original meaning and spiritual significance of the word, which Edgar Cayce has emphatically stated to be the highest means of spiritual attunement.

The Mantras or chants are properly sung *O-o-omm*, *O-o-o-mm*, *Hareeee O-o-o-mm*, aloud to begin, then continued silently. If these words are sufficiently stimulating, there is no need of uttering or meditating on any other name or affirmation. This greatest of the Mantras, the *Word*, becomes the pathway to God (as it is said that "Word became flesh and dwelt among us"). Although it is quite normal that the average person may not rise to the highest level of meditation directly, he is sure to experience "the Peace of God which passeth all understanding."

Other expressions, which are spiritual aids during meditation are: *Ram (Raam)*, God, Christ, Krishna, Jesus, *Harē Raam*, *Harē* Krishna, *Harē Krist* or Christ, *Soham* (I Am He), *Harē* Jesus, *Tadham* (I Am That), *Shiv*, *Allah-Hu-Akbar*, *Buddhoham*, *Ahura Mazda*, *Satnam*, *Wahguru*, *Radhaswami*, *Yaweh*, *Shivoham*.

A close American friend of mine, the physician and humanitarian, Dr. William O. McCabe, has reported to me that during his observation and care of terminally ill patients, he has, on many occasions, heard Christians uttering *Om* at the time of death. Obviously *Om*, the highest name of God, is not the creation of any particular culture or religion.

Other names suggested above refer to the manifestations of God incarnating Himself through the *Avataras*. The name of a specific *Avatara*, used by a longing devotee, may serve to bring the person into the presence of God in that particular form. However, one who meditates continuously ultimately rises above all the specific forms. For him there is no difference among Rama, Krishna, Jesus, *Ahura Mazda, Allah,* or *Wahguru.*

The novice may choose any of the names and use it for one week. The initial choice, made intuitively, is likely to be the proper one. It should lessen all tensions, increase a sense of love and result in the seeing of inner light. If the name selected is not suitable and the progress is slow, one should choose another. For some names are more helpful than others for different individuals.

In His pure essence or spirit, God is above all names. But His manifestation in name and form, in sound and light, as described in all religious scriptures, is real, just as the *Avataravada* is a real manifestation. For our time, the refuge in name or *Nama* is an essential step, a vehicle to transport us from the spatiotemporal world to our divine dwelling place. Thus, the utterance of the name, during the meditation, must be continuous, with ears always alive to hear the Sound, and the closed eyes always eager to see the Light.

To begin, assume the seated posture, tightly close the ears with the thumb of each hand, press the eyelids with the first two fingers, and turn the gaze of the eyes inward to the center of the forehead. This posture cannot be held for very long, because the body must be erect and still. Therefore, after five or ten minutes the hands may be removed, but silent meditation on the name and concentration on the light which one will experience should continue undisturbed. The silent name is essential in withdrawing the mind from all distractions and attracting the soul to the Cosmic Consciousness of Grace and Love.

The preparation period merges into the highest stage of the attunement or *Samadhi*. There are three levels of *Samadhi* or yoga. *Dharana*, the stage of attention, consists in withdrawing the consciousness from all diffuse external and internal objects and ideas and fixing the mind on a selected one. At this stage attention may be either external or internal. In external attention, one's gaze may be fixed on a candle light, a picture, a flower, or other focal point. This exercise should be practiced in isolation. In internal attention, a thought, prayer, or affirmation may be selected and repeated vocally in low voice, with eyes closed.

Dhyana, the second stage, is inner concentration. Eyes must be closed and some image—of Jesus Christ, Rama, Krishna, or even a geometric form—should be mentally projected and the whole attention focused on it. Neither of the first two stages should be prolonged, because both are merely preparation for entering into the depths of the soul. After some practice the second step may be eliminated, graduating directly from the first stage to meditation proper.

Meditation proper or *Samadhi* is the actual at-onement with the Maker. Here there are two levels. In *Samprajnata Samadhi* the subject remains self-conscious and the experience of Sound and Light is such that the knower and the known, the seer and the seen maintain their differentiation. It is here that the silent utterance of the name must continue. This stage automatically enters into the climax of *Asamprajnata Samadhi*, which transcends all contradictions, differences, disharmonies, and even the distinction between the knower and the known. It is a state of pure Being. But it is a real ultraempirical experience of the totality of the Soul—the Self—Christ-consciousness—God-consciousness—Perfection—as long as it lasts. The effects of this communion on the normal level of consciousness produce an ideal integration of the body, mind, intellect, and soul, resulting in health, happiness, and harmony in the total human personality.

11 ❧
Beyond Karma and Reincarnation

The climax of *Samadhi* is the most intensely natural experience of man as Soul. Although it is indescribable to the person who has not personally known it, it is not supernatural, something other than nature. Rather, it is *supra*natural, rising above the material and even intellectual nature of all beings. The highest stage of this spiritual experience is the earned prize of physical, ethical, and spiritual effort, the actualization of the spiritual potential. As one of the Cayce readings states, "Each soul enters the material plane for the manifestation of its individual application of an ideal in respect to the Creative Forces or Energies. For there are no short cuts to knowledge, to wisdom, to understanding—these must be lived, must be experienced by each and every soul."

What is the "wisdom or understanding" to be gained by the "application of an ideal to the Creative Forces or Energies, which must be lived and must be experienced by each and every soul"? We have already established that self-realization is attainable through disciplined meditation. In addition, the effects experienced during *Samadhi* continue visibly in day-to-day life, and the aspirant gradually becomes free of relativities and dualities. He undergoes the same experiences as unenlightened souls do; eats the same food; takes the same drink; has the same feelings and emotions and enjoys the same intellectual pursuits. But in every experience he has the advantage of an extra delight, which makes him immune to frustration, because he is not attached to the senses and the intellect. His knowledge becomes wisdom. His understanding becomes insight, *Jnana*, or inspired intuitive apprehension. The term *Jnana* is in contrast to the word *Vijnana*, which can be broadly translated as science.

The purpose of science is to arrive at the truth through analysis and experimentation. The function of religion is to bring about *Jnana* or enlightenment of the individual by awakening the soul. This is the discovery of the "kingdom of God within," the real conversion, baptism or rebirth. All the manifestations of God have preached the path to this goal of self-discovery, the *Moksha*, the *Nirvana*, Resurrection, *Mukti*, or life eternal. But we must distinguish between the two levels of this destination. The first is *Jivan Mukti*, the ultraempirical self-realization, while the soul is within the physical frame, and is still associated with the finite mind and intellect. The second is that of the eternal life, *Videh Mukti*, or complete freedom from all the physical, mental, and intellectual limitations of the material, human, and divine constitutions, since even divine constitution has limitations. The final home of the soul is beyond this level.

While the soul remains within the system of universes, it must be reincarnated either on this earth, or in any other earth of the other solar systems. But when it attains the final release or *Moksha*, reincarnations cease. In other words, the sole purpose of reincarnation is to go beyond reincarnation; the sole purpose of Karma, or action patterns created by the exercise of the free will of the soul, is to go beyond Karma. These laws of the conservation of ethical energy and ethical causation are finally to be transcended by the soul. A person's belief in or understanding of these laws neither absolves a soul from ethical responsibility, nor hinders its final release. Knowledge can hasten the liberation only when this knowledge inspires to the right path of self-realization, which is the forerunner of eternal life. If a person has not experienced enlightenment, if the effects of self-realization have not been observed during the lifetime, an accomplished salvation is an illusion. Millions of persons die with this illusion and are again and again reincarnated.

It is very rare for someone to recall spontaneously a past life, but self-realization is also self-discovery, and recollection becomes commonplace. Once attained, however, memories of past lives which emerge have significance only historically, as relics of the past. The awakened soul rises above history and time because it can experience eternity before entering into Eternity.

Eternity is the true home of the soul—its intended environment. Edgar Cayce has beautifully interpreted the meaning of the birth of the Christ child as the gift of the Way Home:

Let that mind be in thee ever which has prompted thee in thy better self to hold fast to those things that take hold not upon men's fancies for self-indulgences or self-aggrandizements, but that fancy that life and all of its various phases of experience are *real*—and *take hold* upon God as manifested in the Christ-Child, who thought it not robbery to make Himself equal with God, yet put on flesh, even as thee, that He might become the *way* through which man might find His way—*HOME!* Hold fast to that—as is embodied in the whole sound of *H-O-M-E!* (849–18, p. 4).

It is a moving description of the identification of the human soul with Christ, the way. Edgar Cayce has beautifully analyzed that one must "hold fast to that—as is embodied in the whole sound of *H-O-M-E!*" This constant resonance of the word, or sound, through our own self, must be merged with the Universal Self, so that self-discovery, which alone quenches our spiritual longing, may become an immediate fact. There is no doubt that every normal being is in constant search of his own self, his REAL self as Edgar Cayce would term it. This eternal restlessness of the spirit is the cause of his dissatisfaction and frustration, in spite of any other achievements.

Man's incredible material progress has not brought peace of mind or real happiness to him so far, for affluence itself brings complexities to society and to personal relationships. Man is in search of his soul, in search of God, in search of fulfillment and perfection, unaware of the fact that the kingdom of God is within himself. But how does man discover his own greatness? His own true value? Like the woman who hunts frantically and obsessively for her priceless jewels, only to find that she has been wearing them all the while, man searches obsessively in church, society, and possessions, for his missing fulfillment, when it is within him, waiting to be discovered. The propounders of all religions worthy of the name, have revealed man's fallacy, but unfortunately their successors have substituted the form for the essence.

The sages of India discovered the truth after spiritual research of thousands of years and proclaimed, "That thou art," "Know thyself," "I am He," "I am Brahman," "God alone is Truth, all else is nonexistent," and "Everything indeed is replete with God." Jesus Christ said, "The kingdom of God lies within you," and "Love thy neighbor as thyself." These statements have no clear meanings for the nonawakened person. But without understanding these truths, no person can be truly religious.

In one sense, it can be said that just as there are no gods but God, similarly, there are no religions but Religion. Christ-consciousness, the result of spiritual discipline, love, and Grace, is not salvation by blind faith. As long as a person discriminates between men, and even between religions; as long as a person entertains negative, hostile attitudes, and as long as he assumes his right to monopolize God's love, he has not advanced toward Christ-consciousness. Ecclesiastical, intellectual, or academic achievements, worldly authority and power, are irrelevant as evidence of salvation. Even the possession of psychic power is not necessarily indicative of spiritual development, and may do actual harm by encouraging the ego. Edgar Cayce was a unique exception to the usual morbid passivity and egocentricity of psychics, which is why the title for him is not accurately justified. Rather, he was a pragmatic mystic, whose dedication to the well-being of all proved him to be an awakened person. Because these readings came from the divine communion of his soul with God, they touched the core of the truth. As a result his views are consistent, cosmopolitan, logical, and philosophic. The pseudomystics cannot reach the spiritual depths touched by Edgar Cayce; and so their views conflict with science, philosophy, and religion as well as each other.

Unity of goal does not imply unity of approach. Although the Truth is One, the paths are several, and the various religions and denominations, organized and unorganized, exist as stimulating forces which awaken man's spiritual curiosity. The rituals of baptism, confirmation, and particularly communion; the hymns and *Mantras*, incense and candles, have a great effect on the mind of a novice. But they are the means, not the end; not irrevocably structured, but finitely conceived.

In this context, religion is in effect an aid, a lifebelt for a learner. But unless the aid is finally surrendered, the ability to stay afloat independently is never realized. However, once independence is established, the graduate has the responsibility to remain to guide others to the authentic goal, without making distinctions in their introductory methods.

The attitude of equal reverence for all religions, all prophets, and all *Avataras* is the evidence of enlightenment. A proselytizer for one religion who underrates others is truly a missionary, not of God, but of himself. Edgar Cayce has laid great stress on unity of God and universality of love in his readings. Two of his statements read: "And what is the first law? Know, O Israel—know, O Self—know, O Seeker of light—that all power and force of good . . . emanates only from the *One Source!*" (1620-1, p. 3). and, "For all knowledge or all power is of Creative Forces—or God. And it is a law that is love, if man will but embrace and live and manifest same in the daily experience" (1432-1, p. 3).

It is evident in the first of two readings quoted above that Israel stands for the "seeker," the "Self," and not for any community, nation or state. Self is "the seeker of light." It is this self which has to be awakened and converted into the REAL SELF. This conversion is Christ-consciousness, the "kingdom of God within." Once the awakening has been effected, the narrow self is merged into the Universal Self, the son of man is absorbed into the Son of God, and the physical relativities are transcended. The seeker of light becomes the source of light to others, because he is directly connected with the *One Source*.

The word *self* has great significance both in the realm of knowledge and of love. We have been emphasizing throughout, the role of knowledge or enlightenment and of love in the universal sense. The two are necessarily interrelated, for the attainment of true knowledge through meditation is not possible without the practice of love. Thus this application of reverence helps meditation and meditation in turn conveys an attitude of universal love—love of God, the source of infinite Love and Power, and the love of man—the neighbor, the fellow aspirant, the image of God. If one has never truly loved a human being, who is the visible manifestation of God, one can never love God, the invisible Master. The commandment to "love thy neighbor as thyself," has no significance without an understanding of the terms *love* and *self*. Self is the living Christ, God within us, the Way and the Light. Soul or self is neither body, nor mind, nor intellect, but transcends these realms of human personality. Jesus Christ, as the fully awakened Son of God, said, "I am the door: by me if any man enter in, he shall be saved, and shall go in and out, and find pasture" (John 10:9). That Christ is "the door" means that soul, not body, mind, or intellect, is the only entrance to salvation.

Christ's notion of love is another concept which has not been universally grasped by the followers of the "Prince of Peace." In our age we find it appalling to recall that there was a time in the history of Europe when Christians burned Christians alive in the name of Jesus Christ. The crusades and tortures in the name of Christianity are marks of hypocrisy in the name of God, love, and Christ. This is not the fault of Christianity, for in the Sermon on the Mount Jesus emphatically stated, "Ye have heard that it hath been said, Thou shalt love thy neighbour, and hate thine enemy. But I say unto you, Love your enemies . . . and pray for them which . . . persecute you;

That ye may be the children of your Father, which is in heaven" (Matt. 5:43–45).

Perhaps no other word has been so much misunderstood as the word *love*. This concept of feeling means self-identification, seeing the light of the soul in others as well as in our own selves. Love emanates from the soul of the individual, as divine love emanates from God. When a person attunes his soul to God through meditation, the divine love flows through, conveying immunity from all hatred and jealousy. The charge to "love your enemies," then, holds no logical contradiction or psychological paradox, for if the word *love* is emphasized, *your enemies* is automatically cancelled. With love there are no enemies. This law of love, uniquely manifested in the person and life of Jesus Christ, is both the result and also the cause of Christ-consciousness, attainable both through meditation and through the application of the law of love to practical life. One of the Cayce readings states, "What is law? Love. What is love? God. What is God? Law and love. These are as the cycle of truth itself. And wherever ye are, in whatever clime, it's ever the same" (3574–2, p. 2).

This law is the spiritual discipline leading to meditation proper, or yoga. We have already seen how meditation and love are interdependent, and that both are the accelerators of Christ-consciousness, the highest manifestation of the Grace of God. The essential design is that the law of Grace, which cancels all Karmas and lifts the aspirant to the highest level of divine love, is the goal of the soul, which must pass through various incarnations in order that it may reach perfection.

In other words, the law of reincarnation, as set up by God and supported by the law of Karma, is not at all the ultimate principle underlying man's destiny. The pinnacle to be reached is Grace, God-consciousness here and life eternal hereafter. The principles of Karma and reincarnation, however, similar to the other laws of nature in the spatiotemporal world, do help to explain the purpose of human life. They give a philosophical and logical explanation of the existence of suffering and evil, which would otherwise conflict with the concept of a just, omniscient, omnipotent, and omnipresent God. The opponents of the reincarnation theory, grossly neglecting the immense evidence available all over the world, have unwittingly reduced the justice and goodness of God to a mockery, by suggesting that every soul is created freshly with only one opportunity for perfection. One weak compromise denies that the soul is reincarnated, but suggests that the spirit is continued through different souls appearing at different times. The confusion arises because the propounder is ignorant of the difference between spirit and soul. Spirit is the Universal Self, while soul is the individuated self. It is illogical to claim that Universal Self, which is infinite and the image of which is the infinitude in the individuated soul, survives through human *bodies*. Correctly, soul, which is actually spirit limited by the action patterns or Karmas, is the entity which materializes itself in the world. By saying that spirit and not soul is reincarnated, one is asserting that soul transcends spirit.

If it is admitted for the sake of argument that a new soul is joined to every body by God, how can the justice of God be defended in the face of handicaps which these newly created souls have to suffer? If God has set the laws of nature in the physical realm, the laws of Karma and reincarnation are the only explanation of the existence of evil and suffering in the human world. What seems to bother many people is the possibility that their soul ever occupies another body. The love for the individual material body apparently is not easily shaken. One of my students uneasily asked, "How can I ever imagine that my soul ever occupied another person's body?" The answer is that the body is not a person, but is merely used by the immortal soul, as it uses the temporary mental constitution, as the means for spiritual development. While the individual soul continues to have the residue of good or bad actions, it changes bodies, just as a man puts on new attire, having cast off the old.

The fact that the average person does not recall past incarnations is not a handicap, but an asset to spiritual development. To recollect that our best friends and closest relations were once our bitter enemies would cause personal conflicts, hard to overcome. However, the memory of the previous incarnations can be recalled through hypnosis or yoga, and the Cayce readings are filled with information of previous incarnations of thousands of persons. From evidence, it appears that most of the cases in which an individual recalls his or her past birth are those in which death in the immediate past life had occurred suddenly and hence, was untimely. But why should we forget that reincarnation is not the goal, but the process through which souls have to pass to perfection?

Overenthusiastic advocates of the theory should not overemphasize the facts of reincarnation. The episodes must be overcome, not indulged. The only advantage to studying the theory of reincarnation and the doctrine of Karma is to give a metaphysical basis to religion. If it is unprofitable to indulge in ideas of salvation by blind faith, without insight into the nature of the soul and its goal, it is equally harmful to neglect the true purpose of reincarnation by indulging in the stories of past relationships with associates of our present life. One danger of a fragmentary knowledge about rebirth is the possibility of becoming self-indulgent and postponing the acceptance of the right path for the next life. That is the chief motive behind the suppression or lack of emphasis on reincarnation in all religions, even including Hinduism.

The necessity for the law of Karma in man's development must be repealed by the law of Grace. The wheel of reincarnation must be stopped by the adoption of the law of love—the love of God and of man which is the crux of every true faith.

The technique of meditation is the means to this goal, and intense prayer is the means to the goal of *Samadhi*. Individual effort combined with mass prayers quickens the spiritual progress both of the single person and of society, for the individual is a spiritual unit and the congregation's development ultimately depends upon the development of the individual soul. The importance of private prayer is illustrated beautifully by Jesus: "And when thou prayest, thou shalt not be as the hypocrites are: for they love to pray standing in the synagogues and in the corners of the streets, that they may be seen of men. Verily, I say unto you, They have their reward. But thou, when thou prayest, enter into thy closet, and when thou hast shut thy door, pray to thy Father which is in secret; and thy Father which seeth in secret shall reward thee openly" (Matt. 6:5–6).

Jesus himself meditated for forty days before taking up the task of guiding others, and then preached that Christians ought to practice tolerance, contentment, moderation, and self-surrender to God, the virtues which are essential for the preparation for *Samadhi*. That a continuous practice of spiritual discipline for the attainment of self-realization is necessary is evident from the following statement of Jesus Christ:

And why call ye me Lord, Lord, and do not the things which I say? Whosoever cometh to me, and heareth my sayings, and doeth them, I will shew to whom he is like: He is like a man which built an house, and digged deep, and laid the foundation on a rock: and when the flood arose, the stream beat vehemently upon that house, and could not shake it: for it was founded upon a rock. But he that heareth, and doeth not, is like a man that without a foundation built an house upon the earth; against which the stream did beat vehemently and immediately it fell; and the ruin of that house was great (Luke 6:46–49).

What was Jesus telling his listeners and disciples? He emphasized the practice of positive love, tolerance, self-surrender to God and individual communion with God in meditation. The combination of meditation and love, as advocated by the life and teachings of Jesus Christ, is undoubtedly the surest way to enlightenment. The progress may be gradual, but it is sure. The ethical and spiritual preparation should not be resented by a true seeker of God, for as the potential power of the atom becomes actual when its fission is effected under restrained conditions, so the potential Christ-nature of the soul becomes actual under self-controlled ethical and spiritual discipline. A seeker of truth cannot call himself serious and refuse to adopt the rule of life any more than a swimmer can call himself serious and refuse to enter the water. With growth and experience the discipline becomes spontaneous, and resentment gives place to assent and frustration to real inner enjoyment.

At that stage a man sees the Light and Christ everywhere—in every person, place, and thing. He sees the underlying unity, identity, and harmony, which is not visible to the ordinary person. He only loves. He cannot hate. He cannot be jealous. He cannot be annoyed, repelled, frustrated, or fearful. He sees Christ in everything because he has identified his own self with everything that exists. This is the awakening. This is the Christ-consciousness, Krishna-consciousness or God-consciousness. This is the real conversion, which brings entry into the kingdom of heaven.

Whatever has been written in this book has no meaning if the reader does not test the truth with his own experience. If there is no desire to experience the truth, to see God face to face; to become one with the Creative Force, no theory, no philosophy and no logic can ever help the seeker. Grace will not be thrust upon him. He can receive Grace only when he exercises his privilege of free will. As one of the Cayce readings puts it:

Q. Should the Christ-Consciousness be described as the awareness within each soul, imprinted in pattern on the mind and waiting to be awakened by the will, of the soul's oneness with God?
A. "Correct. That's the idea exactly!" (5748-14)

There is no anthropomorphism reflected here, but rather a consistent vision of God as Essence or Ground and also as an immanent Reality, manifested through the cosmic process of physical and spiritual evolution of matter and mind, nature and man, subject and object. The application of Christ-consciousness was expressed in the Cayce statement that "there has been shown the way that the Father is mindful of His children; that these as they appear in the earth—yea, thyself—are a portion of His manifestation. Not as an indefinite force, not as an unconcrete thing, not as just a mist, but just as is manifested not only in the Christ but as . . . He manifests—as a portion of that Godhead that is represented in thee, as *in* thy Mind —then ye become aware that ye are *indeed* a child of the living God, and are in materiality for those purposes of manifesting those very things that are the fruits of the Spirit in thy dealings with thy fellow man. . . . Know that as the Mind is represented by the Christ-Consciousness, it is the Builder, it is the Way, it is the Truth, it is the Light; that is, through the manner in which the Mind is held" (1348–1, p. 2–3).

Love of God through our dealings with our fellowmen is a full-time occupation. We do not know in what form God will reveal Himself to us—perhaps a taxi driver, a grocery clerk, a student, a teacher, a patient, or a doctor. Therefore we glorify God at all times, in all our contacts, overlooking the curt language, the angry face; turning away the critical remark with love.

If the seeker has not yet achieved this level, he must continue his meditation with a voluntary practice of divine Love. The search for God, our Home, our Source, and our Goal is a total commitment, as Edgar Cayce emphasized in one of his most beautiful descriptions of the religious life:

"Thou shalt love the Lord thy God with all thy heart, thy mind, thy body; thy neighbor as thyself." This as He gave is the whole law. There is none above that. And ye may, as He has promised, become aware in thy own consciousness of His abiding presence, by the awarenesses that may come to thee as ye meditate, as ye pray from day to day. . . . For this purpose ye came into this experience; that ye might GLORIFY that consciousness, that awareness of His presence, of His Spirit abiding with thee.   (1348–1, p. 3).

Other Quest books on reincarnation —

The Cathars and Reincarnation
By Arthur Guirdham
A 20th century English girl remembers her 13th century life as a heretic.

Experiencing Reincarnation
By James S. Perkins
A first person account of the technique of reincarnation.

Reincarnation: A Hope of the World
By Irving S. Cooper
An essay on the pure optimism implicit in this concept.

Reincarnation
By Leoline L. Wright
What reincarnates, and why don't we remember our past lives?

Reincarnation: An East-West Anthology
Ed. & Comp. by Joseph Head & S.L. Cranston
Quotes from the world's famous figures on rebirth.

Reincarnation: Fact or Fallacy?
By Geoffrey Hodson
An inquiry into the evidence of rebirth.

Available from:
Quest Books
306 W. Geneva Road
Wheaton, Illinois 60187